# NO SMALL CHANGE

# NO SMALL CHANGE

## PENSION FUNDS AND CORPORATE ENGAGEMENT

## Tessa Hebb

**ILR Press**
an imprint of
**Cornell University Press**
Ithaca and London

First published 2008 by Cornell University Press

Printed in the United States of America

Hebb, Tessa.
  No small change : pension funds and corporate engagement / Tessa Hebb.
      p. cm.
  Includes bibliographical references and index.
  ISBN 978-0-8014-4696-2 (cloth : alk. paper)
  1. Pension trusts—Investments—United States. 2. Investments—Moral and ethical aspects—United States. I. Title

  HD7105.45.U6H43  2008
  332.67'2540973—dc22

                                        2008012054

Cornell University Press strives to use environmentally responsible suppliers and materials to the fullest extent possible in the publishing of its books. Such materials include vegetable-based, low-VOC inks and acid-free papers that are recycled, totally chlorine-free, or partly composed of nonwood fibers. For further information, visit our website at www.cornellpress.cornell.edu.

Cloth printing 10  9  8  7  6  5  4  3  2  1

*For Bill*

# Contents

# Acknowledgments

Many people ask me why I look at pension fund investment activity and its impacts on financial markets and the firms they invest in. What makes pension funds so important? My answer is the same as that of the famous U.S. bank robber Willie Sutton when asked why he robbed banks, "because that's where the money is."

First and foremost, I want to thank Gordon L. Clark at the University of Oxford. It is fair to say that this book would not have been possible without his insights and support. We worked together to develop most of the conceptual framework presented in this book. We co-published two articles that laid down much of the groundwork, "The Fifth Stage of Capitalism" and "Why Do They Care?" Gordon Clark is enormously generous with his time, energy, and thought. My afternoons in Oxford spent with him in discussion of this research will long be cherished. He and I share a genuine passion for pension fund research and I hope our collaboration will continue.

I would also like to thank my editor Fran Benson at Cornell University Press for her guidance, patience, and support of this manuscript. In addition, the work was strengthened by a number of anonymous reviewers who provided invaluable insights incorporated into the book.

I am grateful to all my colleagues in the United States, Canada, and the United Kingdom, whose unfailing encouragement has meant the world to me, especially Lisa Hagerman, Elaine Bernard, Larry Beeferman, Isla Carmichael, Jack Quarter, Jamie Salo, Terry Babcock-Lumish, and Dariusz Wójcik. Both Terry and Dariusz have been readers and editors, contributors and colleagues. Dariusz also assisted me with the econometric analysis presented in chapter 5 of this book. I thank Taylor Grey for providing me with the CalPERS 2004–2007 Focus List.

I thank Ted Jackson of Carleton University for his boundless encouragement. I also thank various readers and reviewers of my work: Teresa Ghilarducci, Colin Clarke, David Mackenzie, Paul Tracey, Peter Warrian, Brigid Barnett, Ian Dale, Fred Gorbet, and Peter Chapman.

I want to acknowledge and thank two publishers that have granted permission to allow significant excerpts from three prior articles to be included in this work. (1) Pion Limited, London. G.L. Clark and T. Hebb, "Why Should They Care? The Role of Institutional Investors in the Market for Corporate Global Responsibility," first published in *Environment and Planning A* 37 (2005), 2015–31; and T. Hebb and D. Wójcik, "Global Standards and Emerging Markets: The Institutional Investment Value Chain and the CalPERS' Investment Strategy," first published in *Environment and Planning A* 37 (2005), 1955–74. (2) Springer Science and Business Media. T. Hebb, "The Economic Inefficiency of Secrecy," *Journal of Business Ethics* 63 (2006), 385–405.

I am grateful to all those who gave me personal interviews, particularly Sean Harrigan and Dr. Bill Crist. I am also grateful to the California Public Employees Retirement System, and Raj Thamotheram and the Universities Superannuation Scheme for granting me generous access to their organizations for the case studies used in this research. In addition, I would like to thank a group of twenty-seven people, who attended a seminar on pension fund corporate engagement at Oxford in November 2002, for the marvelous insights they provided. I am particularly thankful to the Rockefeller Foundation and Katherine McFate for their support of this work.

I was fortunate in receiving significant funding for my doctoral thesis at Oxford University where this work began. This research greatly benefited from the support of Oxford University's Clarendon Fund, the Finance Program at the Schulich School of Business, York University, and the William E. Taylor Fellowship of the Social Sciences and Humanities Research Council of Canada.

A sincere thank you to my family: Matt, Dee Dee, Maddee, and Dashiell; Ben, Beth and Mia; Nick; Andrea and Robert; Donald, Jennie, William, and Mathew; and, of course, Susy and Martin. I thank my mother Kate Thorne for everything she did for me. My final thanks go to my husband Bill. Your love, support, strength, and generosity have made it possible for me to pursue my dreams. Without you, none of this would have been possible.

# NO SMALL CHANGE

# 1.
# Understanding Pension Fund Corporate Engagement

Pension funds are not the new moral conscience of the twenty-first century, but they are significant owners of today's corporations. They are also institutions that pay out retirement benefits over long periods of time. Think of the twenty-five-year-old worker who retires at age sixty-five and draws his pension for the next twenty years. Given the length of such commitment, pension funds have to carefully consider companies they invest in over a long period of time and be increasingly aware of the long-term risks from the environmental, social and governance (ESG) factors in their investment portfolio.

Few risks are greater than the environmental risks companies face today. Considering that eight of the last ten summers in the United States were the warmest on record (Gore 2006), it is not surprising that investors are asking companies how they plan to manage climate change risk over time. The same holds true for social risks such as exposure to conflict zones, as is the case in the Sudan, or the potential reputation-ruining risk Wal-Mart is facing from numerous employee lawsuits. Anticipation and mitigation of long-term risks is key to pension fund corporate engagement. A growing number of pension fund trustees and managers have come to believe that, in the long run, ESG considerations lower the risks associated with an uncertain future. They believe companies that behave with certain ESG ethical standards maintain, and even gain, value over time.[1] To this end, pension funds are increasingly engaging companies in their investment portfolio in an effort to raise their ESG standards.

Two forces converged in the late 1990s and early 2000s that strengthened the role of institutional investors.[2] The first was their newfound willingness to act in coalition. The second was the combination of increasing managerial excesses and declining stock values. While absentee owners were seen as part of the problem, renewed corporate governance and managerial oversight by share-holders were touted as the panacea to cure the ailing markets (Deakin 2005).

In widely held capital markets, such managerial oversight by shareholders is possible when large institutional investors aggregate the authority of previously dispersed beneficial owners. Pension funds are increasingly playing this role.

There are two types of pension funds. One is the defined benefit (DB) plan, which pays the retiring plan members based on years served and salary earned. The other is the defined contribution (DC) plan, where retirement payments are based on the amount of annual contributions. These differences are important in determining whether a pension fund will use corporate engagement.[3] Pooled DB pension plans, administered by boards of trustees are able to act as unitary economic agents within capital markets. As a result they lower the transaction costs of monitoring firm-level behavior. In contrast, the individualized nature of DC pension plans makes such actions difficult, though not impossible.

Although both types of pension funds hold significant assets ($9.4 trillion), DC plans are growing while DB plans are shrinking. In 1979 DB plans accounted for 62 percent of all U.S. pension fund participants. By 2005 that percentage had shrunk to 10. For DC plans (401-K plans) the numbers of participants grew from 16 percent to 63 percent over the same period (EBRI 2007).

The same trend is evident with pension plan assets. In 1985 66 percent of total pension assets were held in DB plans, and 34 percent were held in DC plans. By 1996, DC plans held half the total pension assets. From then on DC plans have outpaced DB plans in both numbers and size. By 2005 DC plans held 61 percent of all pension plan assets (Conference Board 2007).

In absolute terms the current assets of large, DB pension plans continue to dominate financial markets. Of the two hundred largest pension plans in the United States, 80 percent of the assets are held by DB plans (Pension and Investments 2007). This may well be the apex of Anglo-American, trusteed, defined benefit pension plans' growth and thus influence within the financial market. The power of these pension plans may wane in the future, but with assets totaling $2.7 trillion their size makes them effective in influencing firm-level decisions.

Within the pension fund universe, there are public sector pension funds, private corporate funds, and Taft-Hartley or multi-employer funds. With only a few notable exceptions private corporate funds do not become active owners and do not use corporate engagement to raise the standards of firms in which they invest. In most cases these corporate-sponsored funds do not exercise scrutiny over other corporations, fearing that will bring the same treatment in return. This means a considerable amount of U.S. pension fund assets (close to $5 trillion) are not used for active ownership.[4]

Most U.S. "activist" pension funds tend to be large DB funds in the public sector where these plans continue to grow. These funds increased in absolute size from $200 billion in 1980 to $2.7 trillion in 2005. As a share of total institutional investment, activist public employee funds rose from 7 percent to 11 percent.[5] That said, not all activist funds are drawn from this pool. TIAA-CREF, with $437 billion (as of September 2007) assets under management for colleges and universities, is the best example of an activist DC private plan in the United States.[6]

A key actor among the activist DB pension funds is the California Public Employees Retirement System (CalPERS), the largest U.S. DB pension fund, with assets totaling $245 billion as of June 2007. CalPERS and other activist pension funds are leading the attempt to shift power away from corporate managers back to shareowners.[7] This book traces CalPERS' corporate engagement strategies beginning with its activist stance on corporate governance in the 1980s through 2007.

Activist pension funds are shifting the power dynamic between owners and managers. In the past, the cost of corporate engagement, when measured against possible gains, meant that few minority shareholders were willing to monitor corporate management. But today's pension funds hold such large stakes in individual firms that they are able to bear these costs alone and, more important, act in coalition with other pension funds. As a result, corporate engagement is a potent force in representing owners' interests in today's companies. This new representation is changing the principle–agent debate (Clark and Hebb 2004).

Previously owners have been widely dispersed and therefore essentially powerless to control corporate managers and boards (Berle and Means 1933). But the large holdings of pension funds and their newly found ability to form coalitions mean that corporate engagement is a potent force in aligning managerial interests with those of shareholders.

Such coalitions are possible because changes in securities laws allow for easier communication between shareholders and because transaction costs of both monitoring and coordinating responses have been lowered when measured against the increases in share value such activity generates. In the past pension funds were deemed ineffective as corporate monitors, and were identified as "lone wolves" in their attempts to provide oversight of corporate decision making. In the early 1990s this tendency toward isolation was seen as the major drawback to pension funds' effectiveness as corporate monitors (see, for example, Coffee 1991, 1997; and O'Barr and Conley 1992).

Although CalPERS and other large activist pension funds are important individual players, it is the institutional investor coalitions that have the greatest opportunity to influence and engage corporate management. From 1980 to 2005 U.S. institutional investors increased their holding of outstanding U.S. equities from 37 percent to 61 percent. By 2005 activist state and local funds held close to 10 percent of all U.S. equity. Thus when these funds act in coalition they wield considerable influence.

Given their history as "lone wolves" it is little wonder we see some tensions in these large institutional investor coalitions. While prepared to act in coalition, pension funds simultaneously seek to keep their own management costs as low as possible and therefore resent the "free riders" who benefit from increased corporate standards but do not bear the costs of the endeavor. "Making the interventions in the investment system that will have the maximum positive impact over the next decade calls for asset owners and their investment advisors to undertake a steep learning curve and above all, to collaborate far more effectively then they have to date" (Thamotheram and Wildsmith 2007, 443).

There is an increasing number of effective coalitions on which to model future action by these key actors. These new coalitions cluster around ESG issues. The Carbon Disclosure Project (CDP) representing $41 trillion in assets (as of February 2007), the United Nations (UN) Principles for Responsible Investment (PRI) with signatories representing $8 trillion (as of April 2007), Institutional Investors for Climate Risk, and Coalition for Environmentally Responsible Economies (CERES) are four examples of effective coalitions working on environmental standards. The Extractive Industry Transparency Initiative and the Sudan Campaign are two examples of coalitions of investors focused on social issues. The Council of Institutional Investors and the International Corporate Governance Network are two long-established corporate governance coalitions. All of these institutional investor coalitions have strong records of success in influencing companies to raise their standards. Most use some form of corporate engagement to achieve their goals.

At its best corporate engagement offers a long-term view of value that both promotes higher environmental, social, and governance standards and adds share value, thus providing long-term benefits to future pension beneficiaries. At its worst it diverts the attention of pension fund officials from their primary responsibility of ensuring the retirement benefits of their members, and encourages pension funds to usurp the rightful responsibilities of corporate managers. This book examines corporate engagement and its impacts on firms in an effort to see how the potential from this newly emerging force is being realized.

## Pension Fund Power

Pension funds and other institutional investors have been growing in size and influence in financial markets since the 1980s. Collectively U.S. institutional investors hold $24 trillion in assets and control $11 trillion in equities, roughly 60 percent of outstanding equities in the United States (Conference Board 2007). Of those equity holdings, pension funds hold $5 trillion, and activist state and local pension funds hold $2 trillion.

In the 1980s and 1990s most pension funds behaved no differently from the rest of the financial market. They pushed companies to deliver a steady stream of quarterly earnings in order to meet standard industry benchmarks. But as pension funds grew, they lost their ability to sell stock when dissatisfied with performance (a practice known as the "Wall Street Walk").

Three trends directly affected the ability of pension funds to sell corporate stock when they were unhappy with financial or corporate performance. First, their sheer size meant pension funds held large equity positions that made them increasingly vulnerable to the performance of the market as a whole. This phenomenon has been dubbed the "Universal Owner" (see Hawley and Williams 2000 and 2007).

Second, during the 1990s many pension funds began to use passive stock indexes (such as the Standard and Poor's 500) for their equity investments. As a result they could no longer sell stock because it was part of a broader index in their portfolio. The trend toward indexing grew during the 1990s with stock markets returning 20 percent and more on an annual basis. It became increasingly difficult for active money managers to "beat" the market, particularly once their fees were taken into consideration. Many pension funds moved from active money management to passive money management in the belief that it is hard to pick stocks that consistently outperform the market as a whole.

Third, selling large holdings can result in lower stock prices, a practice that would run counter to pension funds' fiduciary responsibility. As Georg Siemens, the nineteenth-century founder of Deutsche Bank, said, "If you can't sell, you have to care" (cited in Monks 1995, 1).

Because these three trends are driven by pension fund size, CalPERS and other large pension funds took advantage of this phenomenon first. Pension funds realized that key to their fiduciary duty was a long-term view of value within their investment portfolio (Freshfields Bruckhaus Deringer 2005). CalPERS incorporated the concept of long-term value into its core Principles of Corporate Governance: "Corporate directors and management should have a long-term strategic vision that, at its core, emphasizes sustained shareowner value. In turn, despite differing investment strategies and tactics, shareowners should encourage corporate management to resist short-term behavior by supporting and rewarding long-term superior returns" (CalPERS 2007b).

However, a long-term view of value remains a somewhat difficult task for pension funds and their money managers who still rely on quarterly earnings reports as indicators of "success," and in a period of declining equity premiums many short-term investment practices are being utilized that are hard to marry with the pension funds' stated long-term investment philosophy.[8]

Pension fund managers must inevitably be concerned with both short-term returns, as part of the benchmarking process fundamental to fiduciary duty, and long-term value, as expressed through raising firm-level accountability, transparency, social and environmental standards.[9]

In the past, many researchers found pension funds to be dominated by short-term, myopic investors whose impatience often eroded share value (Bushee 1998; Romano 2001; Shleifer and Vishny 1988). But these findings were based on short-term examinations of stochastic shocks measured around specific corporate announcements rather than examinations of pension fund investment behavior over longer time horizons (Bauer et al. 2003).

Pension funds have been found to have a lower stock turn over rate when compared to other institutional investors (Brancato 1994). Other studies indicate that pension fund investors value long-term investment in research and development as well as other capital expenditures (Jarrell et al. 1985; Majunder 1994; Marsh 1990; McConnell and Muscarella 1985). Pension fund managers are prepared to reward analysts who consider environmental, social, and governance factors in their analysis. The Enhanced Analytics Initiative (EAI) whose signatories manage $2.4 trillion of assets, is a good example of the trend toward a long-term view of value. Signatories to the EAI commit a percentage of their analysts' mandates to those who use extra-financial as well as financial criteria in investment selection (Thamotheram and Wildsmith 2007).

## Pension Fund Corporate Engagement Drivers

Pension fund corporate engagement is a legitimate use of the owners' rights in a company to provide oversight and protect shareholder value. But it does not mean that owners interfere in day-to-day management decision making. What activist pension funds seek from management is greater accountability to shareholders, greater transparency, and higher standards of corporate behavior.

Corporate engagement itself can range from quiet discussions with management and the voting of proxies to more contentious approaches such as mounting dissident shareholder resolution campaigns and public removal of firms and even whole countries from investment portfolios.

Corporate engagement does not ask companies to sacrifice long-term profitability. It seeks higher corporate standards in order to reduce risk over time. Though such corporate standards are often referred to as corporate social responsibility (CSR), it is important to note that pension fund corporate engagement concerns itself solely with the long-term interests of shareholders. Although corporate engagement aligns corporate managers with shareholders' long-term interests, CSR suggests that companies respect all their stakeholders including clients, employees, community, governments, suppliers, and customers, as well as its shareholders. In contrast, many pension fund investors argue that greater regard for the long-term and increased corporate social responsibility reduces risk, adds share value, and in the end serves shareholders' interests.

The first driver of pension fund corporate engagement is the growing asset size. Large holdings alone would not be sufficient to foster corporate engagement, but it would be when combined with a long-term investment horizon and active ownership.

Throughout most of the 1990s, the bull market roared through the Anglo-American financial system, reinforcing the myth of the "new economy" and its attendant stock market riches. The 1990s also witnessed the impact of huge pension fund investors who were active in financial market decisions. Although the power and potential influence of pension funds was present through the boom, for the most part pension fund trustees and money managers used their market position in very conventional ways.

However, following the 2000 collapse of the technology, media, and telecommunications (TMT) stock bubble and the corporate governance scandals of 2001 and 2002, there was a shift toward pension funds' need for long-term value. This shift is marked by two changes in investment behavior. The first is a shift in investment style—away from "growth" and toward "value" investing. The second is increased awareness among pension fund investors regarding their apparent short-term myopia and the prospects for a longer-term investment horizon necessary to realize increased share price from "value" investing.

The second driver of pension fund corporate engagement is the amount of assets held in passive indexes that restricts pension funds' exit from companies that have poor standards or are underperformers in the market. In 1984, two hundred largest DB pension funds in the United States held only $50 billion in passive index funds; twenty years later this amount had grown to almost $800 billion (see figure 1.1).

With the phenomenal run up of the stock market in the 1990s it became increasingly difficult for money managers to "outperform" the stock market.

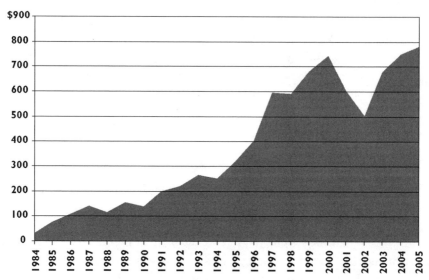

**Fig. 1.1 Growth of indexed assets of the top two hundred
U.S. defined benefit plans (billions)**

*Source:* Pensions and Investments (2006).

Consequently, many pension funds, including CalPERS, moved increasing amounts of assets into passively managed index funds that mirrored the market. The Standard and Poor's 500 Index, comprising the largest five hundred companies in the United States by market capitalization, had annual growth rates of 20 percent during this period (see figure 1.2). However, owning an index fund means you must hold every company in the index. As a result pension funds were not able to sell stock of individual companies even when unhappy with their governance or financial returns.

Corporate engagement's third driver is found in the growing evidence of a correlation between strong environmental, social, and governance standards, and share value outperformance (see Gompers et al. 2003, Anson et al. 2003). Increasingly pension fund investors look to ESG indicators as proxies for long-term performance. These factors are sometimes referred to as extra-financial as they are often not part of the required annual financial statements and filings. Some companies have chosen to report separately on these issues as part of their voluntary corporate social responsibility or CSR reports. Because pension funds and other institutional investors see these factors as bearing on risk there is increased pressure to have them included in the mandatory annual statements as material to companies' performance.

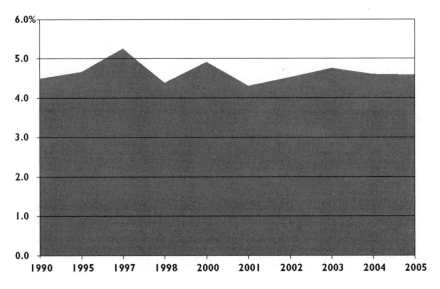

**Fig. 1.2 Indexed assets of the top two hundred U.S. defined benefit plans as a percent of U.S. market capitalization**

*Source:* Pensions and Investments (2006), and U.S. Government Statistics.

Thus, ESG issues would be part of the material disclosures in corporate annual reports.

Measuring extra-financial corporate behavior used to be the domain of a few boutique rating agencies. But interest in these aspects of corporate behavior is becoming more mainstream with rating companies such as Standard and Poor's, Moody's and Fitch establishing metrics by which to measure corporate environmental, social, and governance standards of firm behavior. Not only do activist pension funds rely on ratings agencies for analysis of the risks from these extra-financial indicators for investment decision making, they also use rating agency reports to indicate opportunities for corporate engagement.

The fourth driver of pension fund corporate engagement is the increasing amount of international equity held by pension funds (see figure 1.3). In 2005, the largest twenty-five U.S. pension funds held close to 14 percent of their assets in international equity.[10] With increased international exposure, long-term pension fund investors are becoming sensitive to the need for companies to conduct business in the framework of global standards.

Equally dramatic is the increase in pension fund investment in emerging markets around the world where ESG risks are often greater than in more developed markets (see figure 1.4).

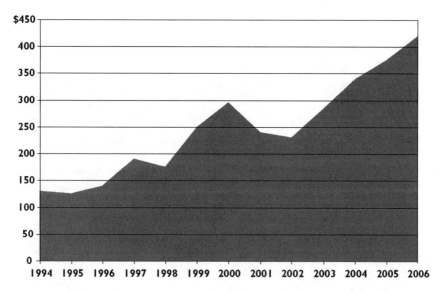

**Fig. 1.3 Growth of international equity assets of the top two hundred U.S. pension funds (billions)**

*Source:* Pensions and Investments (2007).

Previously, pension fund corporate engagement on international social and environmental concerns was limited to single issues such as the South African divestment campaign of the 1970s and 1980s (examined in greater length in chapter 2). Often these campaigns were driven by legislative demands rather than by the pension funds themselves. Over the past twenty years some U.S. state legislatures have mandated pension funds to divest from South Africa, from tobacco products, and since 2005, from the war-torn Sudan. Pension funds are within their fiduciary duty to divest these stocks from their portfolio (*Board of Trustees vs. City of Baltimore* 317 Md. 72, 562, A.2d 720 [1989]) and state legislatures are increasingly making such demands. By 2007, eighteen U.S. state legislatures had called for their state pension funds to divest from companies doing business in Sudan.[11]

Three initiatives highlight the influence investors have internationally: CDP, UNEP PRI, and the Extractive Industries Transparency Initiative (EITI). The CDP asks institutional investors to support a request for greater corporate disclosure of greenhouse gas emissions. As of February 2007 this initiative had signatories representing $41 trillion of assets globally (Carbon Disclosure Project 2007). The influence of this initiative is being felt by corporations because of the greater transparency requirements and the need for increased

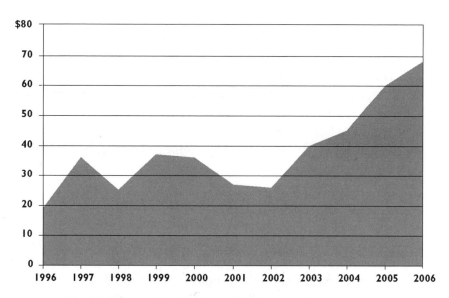

**Fig. I.4 Growth of emerging market market equity assets of the top two hundred U.S. pension funds (billions)**

*Source:* Pensions and Investments (2007).

sensitivity to their impact on global climate change. The newly formed UN PRI (2007), with signatories representing $8 trillion of assets, proposes a set of guidelines for investors seeking to advance long-term sustainable global markets. Meanwhile the EITI calls for greater transparency in the global extractive industries with a particular emphasis on reducing bribery in emerging markets around the world. All three initiatives are new, global, represent large coalitions, and address the social and environmental concerns of institutional investors. All three initiatives seek greater transparency from corporations and use corporate engagement as their preferred form of interaction. These initiatives are part of pension funds long-term investment strategies and are prime examples of pension fund corporate engagement at work.

Given the growing power of pension fund international investment flows, it is little wonder that global activists see pension funds as potential points of leverage to reach global equity and social justice goals. A new generation of international activists is drawing the world's attention to the deepening divide between developed and developing nations and more explicitly, the growing gap between the world's wealthy and the world's poor. The protests against the World Trade Organization, World Bank, and International Monetary Fund in the late 1990s showed that many believed the goals of social justice, equality, human rights, labor rights, and environmental standards to be unattainable in the rush to serve the needs of global capital.[12] However, since 2002 there has been a growing realization that global capital flows can indeed become a useful tool if investment is harnessed to meet demands for sustainability and global social justice.

Much as we saw during the anti-apartheid divestment campaign of the 1970s and 1980s, the line between long-term financial benefit and social action is being blurred by global pressure to respond to social justice issues around the world. Chapter 5 provides evidence from CalPERS' emerging market screening that backs this claim.

## Corporate Engagement Typology

There is a hierarchy of steps through which most pension funds progress as they engage corporations. These steps range from the simplest and easiest activities to the most complex and contentious. Typically it takes pension funds a number of years of active ownership to work through all ten steps (see table 1.1).

---

**Table 1.1    Ten steps of corporate engagement**

---

1. Develop policy statement

2. Identify areas of major concern in corporate governance, environmental and/or social conduct.

3. Develop proxy voting guidelines and vote proxies in a manner that addresses concern.

4. Take membership in coalitions of institutional investors.

5. Where relevant, include formal codes of governance, social and environmental conduct that address these concerns in proxy voting guidelines.

6. Engage company officials on extra-financial issues identified above.

7. Consider extra-financial factors in investment selection and monitoring.

8. Consider extra financial factors in fund management selection and monitoring.

9. Relationship investing.

10. Propose minority shareholder resolutions and develop Focus Lists.

---

To be successful both the pension fund board of trustees and its senior management must agree to undertake corporate engagement. Each must understand its impact on long-term investments. Without the commitment of both sets of key actors, corporate engagement can become a mere box-ticking activity by fund managers, rather than a way to use owners' influence to raise the environmental, social, and governance standards of companies.

This box-ticking tendency was evident in the United Kingdom, where government legislation requires pension funds to say whether and to what extent they use environmental, social, and ethical standards in investment decision making. With the advent of the legislation in 2000, few pension funds wanted to be excluded. Sixty percent of UK funds indicate they used these standards to judge investment (Mathieu 2000). However, when asked how they used them, over two-thirds replied that they instructed their fund managers to take these aspects of the firm into consideration to the extent that it *did not* impact immediate shareholder value.

Table 1.1 details the steps most pension funds progress through as they engage corporations. In order to begin the process of engagement pension funds take the first step of establishing a policy statement that guides their activity. These statements or policies are developed at the board level of the fund. They are often referred to as policies of responsible investment and are part of the overall statement of investment principles that guide the fund.

Such statements are further refined in step two of pension fund corporate engagement. Here pension funds identify the area of corporate behavior they are seeking to change through engagement. Research indicates that most pension funds identify corporate governance issues when they begin the process of engaging corporations. This area is natural for pension fund investors, as all shareholders have legal rights that allow them input into the governance of corporations. In 2007, many activist pension funds sought a "say on pay" and engaged corporations on the compensation offered senior management. For the first time a "say on pay" shareholder proposal won majority support at a publicly owned U.S. company when 50 percent of shareholders voted to have future compensation packages at Verizon submitted to a non-binding shareholder vote.[13]

It is important to note that several research studies including one by Harvard Business School link strong standards of corporate governance with positive financial performance over time (Gompers et al. 2003).

Standard areas of behavior identified by pension funds for corporate engagement include greater accountability measures such as the separation of board chair from CEO, limits on executive compensation, and nomination of board members. They also incorporate greater transparency from corporations on social and environmental issues. Chapter 3 examines the increasing shift toward transparency demands in pension fund corporate engagement, while chapters 4 and 5 detail investors' interest in the social and environmental standards of corporate behavior.

Once the pension fund has decided to consistently vote its proxies according to the issues identified in step two, they develop proxy-voting guidelines to govern this activity. This is the third step in pension fund corporate engagement. U.S. pension funds are required by law to vote their proxies, which are seen as a plan asset under ERISA legislation. Although voting proxies is the easiest form of corporate engagement, until 2001 most pension funds and other institutional investors voted their proxies in accordance with management's wishes. The downturn in the market in 2001 provided a wake-up call to investors. Pension fund investors began to develop detailed guidelines for voting their proxies and increasingly contract proxy-voting services that both advise pension funds and vote their proxies according to these guidelines. Such guidelines cover a range of corporate governance issues. Although social and environmental issues are often dealt with on a case-by-case basis, several large pension funds have developed proxy-voting guidelines that cover these issues. Many pension funds now post both their proxy-voting guidelines and voting records on their websites to provide greater transparency in their own governance mechanisms.

As detailed throughout this book one of the most important shifts in pension fund corporate engagement is the newly found willingness of funds to work together. Once the pension fund has decided to become active owners they seek out others concerned with similar issues (step four in table 1.1). Many pensions funds are restricted in how much of their own portfolio can be in a single holding, as a result they usually hold at most 1 to 2 percent of their own portfolio in any given large public company. CalPERS is no exception. It holds close to $2 billion in General Electric (GE) stock and debt, which for the $245 billion pension fund is its largest holding (as of December 2006). For GE this figure represents only .5 percent of total market capitalization. GE's primary concern lies with satisfying the other 99.5 percent of their shareholders. When pension funds and other institutional investors act in concert, however, they can represent upward of 10 percent or more of a company's holdings. It is at this point that corporate engagement becomes a potent force. Coalitions on corporate governance issues include the U.S. Council of Institutional Investors and the International Corporate Governance Network. Increasingly coalitions of institutional investors have formed on a number of social and environmental concerns, such as the Institutional Investors on Climate Risk, the CDP, the EITI and the signatories to the UN PRI.

In step five, pension fund investors integrate formal codes of behavior adopted by coalitions such as the OECD Codes of Corporate Governance or Guidelines for Multinational Enterprises, the CERES Environmental Standards, the Global Sullivan Principles, or the McBride Principles into their proxy-voting guidelines. As a result, when a minority shareholder resolution calls for a company to adopt these codes of conduct, the pension funds vote in favor of the resolution if the code is relevant to the companies business.

Once pension funds are actively voting their proxies and participating in coalitions, they begin to engage companies directly (step six). This type of engagement is usually done through private channels and is therefore hard to quantify. Phone calls, letters, and private meetings are all employed as pension fund investors express concern with senior corporate management on issues they believe could have a negative impact on long-term shareholder value. Most of what is known about this type of engagement is anecdotal with either corporate executives or pension fund officials revealing these interactions. Such engagement is not designed to inflict reputational damage on the corporation, but rather to privately convey concerns to management with the hope that the latter will respond voluntarily to the request from a significant shareholder or group of shareholders. Research indicates that when the shareholder is large and influential with significant holdings in the company, management is more likely to respond positively to such engagement.

Ultimately in order for such quiet engagement to work there must be some threat from shareholders if the company refuses to change its behavior. Such threats are usually to the reputation of the company. In most cases senior management fear negative publicity and will often engage rather than run the risk that investors will use the media or mount a dissident shareholder campaign to achieve the changes they are seeking.

Generally pension fund investors want to avoid negative publicity, as they do not want to drive down the value of their shareholding but rather to raise the standard of corporate behavior. This is in contrast to socially responsible investors who seek public attention and often mount minority shareholder campaigns based on small amounts of holdings and no initial engagement with the corporation. These investors often use their ownership position to inflict reputational damage even at the expense of shareholder value. For them the change in corporate behavior is a more important goal than long-term share value.

Steps seven and eight—using extra-financial information to select investments and fund managers—take place only when mainstream investment managers accept the importance of extra-financial information in long-term share value. To date most mainstream analysts discount the value of extra-financial data as relevant in investment selection. The investment belief that all information about a firm is already known and incorporated in its current market price is strongly held by both internal and external pension fund money managers and is the view most often taught in business schools around the world. In order to successfully move to steps seven and eight there must be a systematic integration of the importance of extra-financial investment criteria to the pension fund. This means that responsible investing managers are not public affairs officers, but rather are fully integrated in the investment decision making of the pension fund. It also means benchmarking and financial incentives for both internal and external money managers must be geared to long-term rather than short-term investment horizons.

As with standard financial information, money managers rely on rating agencies to provide them with extra-financial ratings of corporate behavior. In addition to small boutique rating agencies, mainstream agencies such as Standard and Poor's, Moody's and Fitch are providing extra-financial ratings for companies' environmental, social, and governance standards. The EAI is an example of institutional investors valuing such extra-financial information. Signatories to the EAI agree to set aside 5 percent of their trading commissions for analysts who use extra-financial information in their investment selection process.[14] By May of 2007 the EAI had members representing $2.4 trillion in assets.

Step nine is termed relationship investing. Here pension funds move beyond simple requests for transparency, disclosure, and factoring extra-financial indicators into investment selection. With relationship investing the investor is prepared to hold a significant stake in the company, usually greater than 10 percent, and often takes one or more board positions as well. Relationship investing requires a positive response from senior management to such shareholder engagement. Often the investors' management skills are seen as adding value to the company. For most pension funds such a commitment to a single investment would require more due diligence than they are prepared to make. However, we are seeing specialized investment vehicles (e.g., San Diego-based company Relational Investing) adopt this approach with their investment portfolio. Pension funds such as CalPERS are major investors in this vehicle and have made returns upward of 33 percent since its inception in late 2002 to December 2005, outperforming its benchmark by 18 percent during that period—a testament to the added value of relationship investing.

The most contentious stage in corporate engagement is step ten—the mounting of minority shareholder resolutions and the development of Focus Lists that single out non-complying companies in order to force them to change their behavior. With this step shareholders use their position and influence to inflict reputational damage on the firm. As a result the pension fund investor or coalition of investors is often characterized as a bully. This step represents the most significant power shift between managers and owners. Management often resents shareholders' power and becomes intransigent in their position when shareholder resolutions are proposed.

Minority shareholder campaigns have two desired outcomes. Either the resolution is able to garner enough support to pass or at least enough support to provide a strong warning to management[15] or it generates negative publicity that has an equally galvanizing effect, particularly if the shareholders are large institutional investors. In 2007, minority shareholder resolutions calling on ExxonMobil to reduce greenhouse gas emissions and Wal-Mart to resolve issues of equity compensation to women and employees of color are good examples of how minority shareholder resolutions can generate negative publicity for corporations even when they do not pass. If management wants to avoid negative publicity they often seek a solution that allows the resolution to be withdrawn before it comes to a vote.

Focus lists identify a group of underperforming companies with serious environmental, social, and governance problems. Both CalPERS and the U.S. Council of Institutional Investors maintain annual Focus Lists of such firms. These lists are designed to generate negative publicity in an effort to change corporate behavior. Chapter 3 provides detail on CalPERS' Focus List and how it is perceived by the companies it targets. When pension funds and other institutional investors use the tools of step ten they are deeply engaged as active owners with the companies in their investment portfolio and are prepared to use their position in financial markets to achieve their goals.

Since 2004, we have begun to see a backlash to shareholder power, particularly in the United States. According to the *Economist*, "What corporate America is facing is a revolution, the end game of which is management-by-referendum" (2007, 15). Despite early optimism in the years immediately following the Sarbanes-Oxley Act, active owners have seen corporate governance power shift back in favor of management. One of the starkest examples is the slowing of access to the proxy for shareholder-nominated board candidates by the Securities and Exchange Commission.

## Conclusion

Pension fund corporate engagement is a new and unfolding tool that has the ability to significantly influence and raise standards of corporate behavior. Understanding its origins, drivers, and impacts is important for assessing whether this force can indeed match the rhetoric that surrounds it. Chapter

2 details the origins of pension fund corporate engagement and highlights its differences with socially responsible investing (SRI) where we find greater concern for the moral and ethical dimension of investment. While there are intersecting interests between corporate engagement and socially responsible investment, they are not the same.

Chapter 3 looks at the role pension funds are playing in setting corporate governance standards for firms. Here we see a power shift underway between owners of firms and the managers who run them. We also find an increased interest in transparency and disclosure as key corporate governance changes pension funds are requesting.

Chapters 4 and 5 examine the social and environmental corporate standards that are important to pension funds. Chapter 4 asks why pension funds care about these aspects of firm behavior. It finds that corporate reputation is critical to long-term share value. Chapter 5 looks at the influence of global standards on pension fund corporate engagement. It draws on CalPERS' 2002 decision to screen its emerging market portfolio based on a broad matrix of ESG risk factors. As one pension fund official noted, "These days presidents fly over Washington and land in Sacramento." Although the impact of this policy has been significant for emerging market countries, in 2007 CalPERS reexamined this policy in light of the losses against benchmark in their emerging markets portfolio. This policy change and its implications are also examined in chapter 5.

This book concludes with a broad exploration of the policy implications of pension fund corporate engagement. It asks whether these giant pools of capital are able to realize their potential to raise the standards of corporations in a global arena.

Pension fund corporate engagement has the ability to use pension funds enormous assets as leverage to raise the ESG standards of the companies in which these funds invest. Such activity is not driven by utopian views of capital markets but rather by enlightened self-interest on the part of these pension fund investors. Long-term investment horizons mean that these investors are increasingly sensitive to the risk in their investment portfolio brought on by poor corporate behavior. Because it is enlightened self-interest that drives the demand for raised standards, pension fund investing can have tremendous impact on corporate behavior. This book explores the evolution of corporate engagement, its impact, and its promise for the future.

# 2.

# Intersecting Interests

Corporate engagement and socially responsible investment (SRI) share similar approaches and techniques in their engagement with corporations. But what is interesting in the convergence between traditional SRI and newfound pension fund corporate engagement is that the same concept embraces two quite distinct and somewhat hostile approaches to corporate control. Each approach has different origins, rationale, and objectives, yet both use ownership rights to wrest control from corporate managers and put it into the hands of shareholders.

In theory, conventional investment decisions are made based on the expected risk-adjusted rates of return with the stream of future earnings embedded in its current price. However, the longer the investment period under consideration with attendant risk and uncertainty attached, the more broadly defined the set of fundamental attributes of the firm must be. As investors' time horizons lengthen, these concerns reflect the need for higher environmental, social, and governance (ESG) standards previously seen as extraneous investment criteria for institutional investors.

Applying extra-financial criteria to investment selection was formerly the purview of individual investors who wished to align their social values and morals with their investment behavior. They believe that the role of the corporation is to serve the interests of society as a whole, and are often prepared to accept reduced rates of return in exchange. By contrast, pension fund investors' fiduciary duty requires them to focus on the financial aspects of corporate engagement. Pension funds use the outcomes of such engagement not as ends in themselves, but as a set of attributes that add long-term share value to the firm. Because the higher standards that arise from such engagement are the same as those sought by traditional SRI advocates, the corporate, social, and/or environmental standards create an intersection of interest between traditional SRI advocates and the newer institutional proponents.

Negative screening and direct shareholder action are the tools most often used by SRI investors. The dual motivation behind negative screening is to maintain ethical standards within one's own portfolio, and to attempt to raise the cost of capital for the shunned firm in an effort to discipline corporate behavior.[1]

It has been suggested that investment screening has a negative impact on performance because it limits maximum diversification in the portfolio. However, most studies indicate that screening does not affect fund returns (Bauer et al. 2002; Margolis and Walsh 2001). In fact, several studies show a positive business case for socially responsible investing. Beginning in 1990 through May 2005, the socially screened Domini 400 Social Index outperformed the Standard and Poor's 500 Index by 65 percentage points. The main contributor to this outperformance was the elimination of tobacco stocks from the Domini 400 Social Index. It can be argued that SRI indexes are sensitive to changes in public opinion on key issues and are therefore early adopters of broader societal changes that come about through government policy changes, legal changes, or changes in consumer behavior. In this way SRI-screened funds can be thought of as slightly ahead of the market as a whole and as a result can deliver outperformance for investors.

Another tool of SRI investors is corporate engagement and direct-shareholder action in proposing and voting on minority shareholder resolutions at annual shareholder meetings. Increasingly screened SRI mutual funds are engaging companies in dialogue as their first means of changing corporate behavior. Only when engagement fails do these funds propose minority shareholder resolutions. Here the goal is desirable social, ethical, or environmental outcomes with limited thought regarding the impact such action has on corporate profitability. Generally the block of shares held by traditional SRI advocates is small, and as a result, even if the minority shareholder resolution is successfully passed, the outcome of the vote has little impact on the individual's SRI investment portfolio, regardless of its potential impact on the firm. These minority resolutions have often been symbolic courses of action and seldom garnered enough votes to change company policies. SRI advocates rely heavily on the negative publicity generated by their actions to discipline corporate behavior. Their hope is that reputational damage inflicted on the firm will either increase the perceived risk in the firm and therefore raise its cost of capital, or result in a loss of consumer confidence.

Although traditional social investment has gained strength in the last twenty years, its presence in the market is dwarfed in comparison to the growth of mainstream institutional investors, particularly pension funds. Pension fund trustees and managers use corporate engagement in sharp contrast to traditional SRI proponents. While traditional SRI brings moral and ethical judgments to bear on corporate behavior regardless of firm-level costs, pension fund corporate engagement reverses the process. These investors judge corporate behavior in light of long-term share value and hence profit maximization. The profit-maximizing approach of pension fund corporate engagement does little to contest Milton Friedman's assertion that "The social responsibility of business is to increase its profits" (1970, http://www.colorado.edu/studentgroups/libertarians/issues/friedman-soc-resp-business.html). What the profit-maximizing approach acknowledges is that for long-term investors extra-financial aspects of firm behavior are key to identifying potential corporate risks. Control of these risks is often a proxy for good management. The social and environmental outcomes demanded by traditional SRI advocates are the same raised standards that are sought through pension fund corporate engagement for long-term profit maximization.

Although neither SRI advocates nor pension fund corporate engagement has adopted the tactics or motivation of the other, each group seeks the same outcomes in terms of raised standards of corporate behavior. However, the cleavage remains on the purpose of the firm in society and on the most effective form of corporate control. This divide creates a, at times, hostile interaction between these two forces. Yet the shared goals of traditional SRI and pension fund corporate engagement offer a unique opportunity to raise the ESG standards of corporate behavior (see Lydenberg 2007).[2]

## The Purpose of the Firm in Society

The divide between SRI proponents and pension fund corporate engagement is centered on a long-standing argument as to the purpose of the firm in society. Put simply, the argument hinges on whether the purpose of the firm is to make profits for its owners or to serve broader social goals and aims.

From the adoption of the first corporations there has been an on-going debate about the purpose of the corporation in society. While many individuals see corporations as "soulless" entities (e.g., Bakan 2004; Galbraith 1967; Hazlitt 1884), others have argued that the pursuit of profit is the engine of progress. For example, Adam Smith famously noted, "it is not from the benevolence of the butcher … that I expect our dinner but from his regard to his own self interest" (1776, book 1, 20).

Socially responsible investing extends as far back as the 1750s when Quaker organizations refused to invest in firms involved in the production of weaponry. In 1928 the Pioneer Fund was one of the first mutual funds in the United States to impose negative screens excluding tobacco- and alcohol-producing companies from its investment portfolio (Becker and McVeigh 2001). By directing their portfolios in this manner early proponents of socially responsible investing aligned their investments with their moral beliefs and with little concern for the profitability of such behavior.

The SRI movement's growth in the 1970s and 1980s was propelled by such issues as the South African anti-apartheid movement, as well as by the anti-nuclear and anti-tobacco campaigns. By the 1990s traditional SRI extended to direct-shareholder action. Ironically, while negative screening means the company stock is shunned, direct shareholder action requires the investor to maintain an ownership stake in the corporation. But for these SRI investors share-ownership, with its attendant set of rights, provides an avenue to impose socially optimal behavior on the firm. Direct shareholder action usually takes the form of proposing and voting on minority shareholder resolutions at annual shareholder meetings. The goal of these demands is to achieve desirable social, ethical, or environmental outcomes rather than corporate profitability.

Religious organizations and concerned individuals with pooled investments in designated SRI mutual funds and unit trusts tend to dominate traditional socially responsible investing. This movement gained strength and popularity in the United States over the past two decades, increasing from $40 billion in 1984 to $2.3 trillion in 2005 (Social Investment Forum 2006). It is estimated that one in every ten dollars invested in the United States has some form of socially responsible criteria attached (Social Investment Forum 2007).

While traditional SRI has grown into a significant force in the past twenty years, pension funds and mainstream institutional investors continue to dominate U.S. financial markets. In 2005 U.S. pension funds accounted for $4.9 trillion of equity (Conference Board 2007). This figure represents close to 30 percent of total U.S. market capitalization. Within the pension fund universe, activist state and local pension funds have been able to play an important role in the corporate governance movement due to their growth in assets and the percentages of equity they hold in their portfolios. From 1980 to 2005 these funds increased their ownership of the U.S. equity market from 3 percent in

1980, to 10 percent in 2005 (see figure 2.1). State and local funds now hold $1.7 trillion in equity (Conference Board 2007). This exposure to equities allows these funds enormous influence, particularly when they work in coalitions (as discussed in the previous chapter). In addition, these funds, as do all institutional investors, hold positions in the largest U.S. companies, where they exert even more influence. In 2005, four of the largest twenty-five U.S. companies had institutional ownership of over 70 percent (Conference Board 2007).[3]

In 2000 and 2001 the value of state and local pension funds' equity holdings as a percentage of U.S. market capitalization declined because of the drop in equity values and subsequent shift away from public equities by these funds. But by 2005 this figure rebounded due to the growth in state and local pension funds absolute size, and to the increase in the amount of assets they hold in equities (currently valued at 64 percent of these funds' portfolios).

In contrast to traditional SRI proponents, activist pension fund trustees and managers can be thought of as "profit maximizers." Under common law, pension funds are prohibited from using socially responsible investment for "profit-sacrificing" behavior. For profit maximizers, in a world of scarce resources, proper allocation is determined through a perfectly efficient market, with shareholders as the recipients of all economic residual returns.

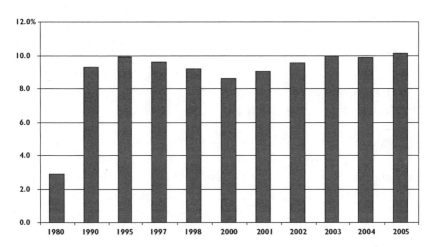

**Fig. 2.1    State and local pension fund equity assets as a percentage
of total U.S. market capitalization**

*Source:* Conference Board 2007, and U.S. PBGC, (2007).

Under these assumptions, unaccountable unelected businessmen (and the few businesswomen) are seen to be the last people who should determine socially optimal outcomes. If firm behavior delivers social "bads" or fails to deliver enough social "goods," profit maximizers believe it is government's role to correct such failures through regulation.

Pension fund investors are bound by fiduciary duty to act solely in the long-term "financial" interest of their beneficiaries. This legal fact requires institutional investors to be long-term profit maximizers. By definition they must reject any profit-sacrificing behavior. This does not mean they reject the use of ESG standards in addition to financial indicators in investment decision making; rather, they reject such behavior as profit sacrificing. Profit maximizers believe in the supremacy of shareholders as the ultimate beneficiaries of corporate activity.

> So long as the company's objective is maximum profits, a concern with the welfare of third parties is necessarily an instrumental one: it is a means of protecting profitability in the long term. The concept of social responsibility, in contrast, demands that the affected interests be treated as ends in themselves, and this will at times require a deviation from long-run profit maximization. (Parkinson 1993, 43)

The profit-maximizing approach of pension fund corporate engagement does little to disturb the orthodoxy of the firm as a nexus of contracts with attendant property rights and profit maximization as its primary objective.

### Corporate Control and Accountability: The Principal-Agent Problem

Although their differing origins and functions can account for some of the past separation between traditional SRI and pension fund corporate engagement, the more obvious contrast lies in their opposing views on both the purpose of the corporation and the means of controlling corporate behavior. The great legal theoretician James Willard Hurst, referring to the uneasy equilibrium between the role of the corporation and public interest said that the impact of large corporations can be accommodated to societal interests either from the outside—through laws, regulation, the market place—or from inside—using its charter, its CEO, its shareholders (1970). Traditional SRI can be described as seeking corporate control from the outside in. In contrast, pension fund corporate engagement can be said to be an inside-out strategy of corporate control.

Both traditional SRI and pension fund corporate engagement recognize the dominant role managers play in determining firm-level activity. As a result, both investment approaches seek owners' control of managers in order to achieve levels of corporate social responsibility that managers would not otherwise select of their own volition. The contrast between traditional SRI and pension fund corporate engagement lies in their differing use of external versus internal agents to influence corporate behavior.

Those who believe the purpose of the firm is the betterment of all society choose external agents of control who derive their power from social rather than corporate sources. Because traditional SRI advocates usually hold only a tiny minority of corporate shares, they use their small investment positions to leverage through the threat of inflicting reputational damage to control corporate behavior. Whether they are divesting from holdings or proposing minority shareholder resolutions, the ultimate intent of their strategy is to generate negative publicity that will in turn shape public opinion. The desired outcome of this strategy is either public pressure on government for regulation, voluntary compliance by firms who fear negative perception of the firm, or consumer boycotts.

A good example of the growing influence of the SRI movement on the government in the 1990s was the screening of tobacco from investment portfolios that helped focus a spotlight on the industry. The government ultimately enacted regulation that required tobacco be declared an addictive substance with corresponding packaging and warning to consumers.

Traditional SRI attempts to enlist voluntary corporate compliance in order to influence management decision making. Today's firms are increasingly conscious of their corporate social responsibility and equally conscious of the investor and consumer pressures to behave in a socially responsible manner. For example, after Shell Oil announced its 1995 decision to sink their oil platform "Brent Spat" in the North Sea, it was threatened by investment and consumer boycotts. The negative publicity generated by these threats to their corporate reputation resulted in Shell's voluntary decision to shelve its plan. Another example is the Sisters of Charity of Saint Elizabeth, who hold a small fraction of Wal-Mart shares, yet have been able to generate significant media attention on Wal-Mart's employment practices. From 2003 to 2006 a variety of shareholder resolutions put to Wal-Mart's annual meetings have resulted in close to 30 percent of non-management votes. The real damage inflicted by these shareholder resolutions has been on the reputation of the company (explored in more detail in chapter 4). But there are limits to the control of corporate managers that external actors can provide. Consequently, traditional SRI has been a weak force in Anglo-American capital markets to date.

In contrast, pension funds hold large established corporate ownership positions with all attending property rights attached. These institutional investors are powerful internal actors and their interest in corporate engagement brings weight to these issues ignored when advocated by traditional SRI proponents. As internal actors they are well within their rights to demand higher standards of corporate behavior.

Pension fund corporate engagement is redefining the Berle and Means paradigm in a new image of corporate control. Adolf Berle and Gardiner Means's 1933 seminal book *The Modern Corporation and Private Property* showed that the twentieth-century rise of public corporations meant a growing dispersal of ownership rights across large segments of the population. They concluded that while the advent of public corporations spread the benefits of capitalism more broadly, owners lost control of firm-level decision making with managers usurping this role.

Pension funds and other institutional investors are able to aggregate the dispersed shareholders of the past. This new concentration of share ownership through institutional investors represents a profound shift in the longstanding corporate control debate (Monks 2001). As a result pension funds use corporate engagement to control firms from inside the corporate structure.

It would be fair to say that control of limited liability companies has been subject to debate almost from their inception. As early as 1776 Adam Smith raised concerns about the inherent danger of separation of ownership from the management of a company's affairs. "The directors of such companies being the managers of other people's money than their own, it cannot well be expected that they should watch over it with the same anxious vigilance with which the partners in a private copartnery frequently watch over their own" (229). This tendency of managers' interests to diverge with those of owners has been described as the principal-agent problem.

The principal-agent problem described above, marks the struggle for corporate control. While owners seek maximum profits, managers who are in control of day-to-day affairs can diverge from owners' interests. Internal control is exerted through shareholders' ability to sell their stock when management diverges from their interests. This creates a market for control, because bad corporate management will ultimately result in selling the firm to new owners who in turn will replace existing managers (Jensen and Meckling 1976).

In the second half of the twentieth century the principal-agent problem has been defined as one of "strong managers and weak owners" (on this topic see particularly Roe 1994). But by 2005 the reality for the twenty-five largest U.S. companies was that 60 percent or more of outstanding stock was held by institutional investors. Average pension fund ownership of these companies was roughly 15 percent. Even in 2000, within the top three firms—Microsoft, General Electric, and IBM—the degree of pension fund ownership concentration was 13 percent, 18 percent, and 17 percent, respectively (Monks 2001, 93). The magnitude of these ownership levels redefines pension fund investing from that of portfolio holdings, closer to the Organization for Economic Cooperation and Development (OECD) definition of direct investors. "The objective of obtaining a lasting interest [which] implies the existence of a long term relationship between the . . . investor and the enterprise and a significant degree of influence on management" (Monks 2001, 84). The OECD benchmark goes on to say:

> Investment in the process through which a minimum—say 10 percent—of the shareholders—exercises influence over the constitutional structuring of portfolio companies. . . . An effective voice in the management, as evidenced by an ownership of at least 10 percent, implies that the . . . investor is able to influence or participate in the management of an enterprise. (84)

Such degrees of institutional ownership may well account for the increasing backlash to corporate engagement. Although early gains were made by activist funds following the 2002 Enron collapse, by 2004 backlash to activist pension funds was already evident. For example, the 2004 election of pro-business Republican Arnold Schwarzenegger as governor of California was quickly followed by a direct assault on the activist pension funds CalPERS (California Public Employees Retirement System) and CalSTRS (California State Teachers' Retirement System). The president of CalPERS board was replaced, which gave a clear signal of the backlash to follow. Both the U.S. Business

Round Table and the U.S. Chamber of Commerce issued media releases of congratulations to Governor Schwarzenegger on the dismissal of the CalPERS president. In a similar vein, David Hirschmann, senior vice president of the U.S. Chamber of Commerce issued a cease and desist letter to New York and Connecticut State pension funds accusing them of "working to advance the social investment agenda of labor." Several State governors suggested that their large defined benefit public employee plans should be terminated in favor of defined contribution plans. The clearest signal of this backlash has been the opposition registered with the Securities and Exchange Commission (SEC) against the proposal to allow access to the proxy for shareholder director nominations. Despite receiving 16,000 responses to the proposal, of which two thirds were positive, the SEC has delayed any further action on this file.

Despite corporate backlash, we are increasingly seeing SRI and pension funds investors working together. Many of today's coalitions include pension funds and other institutional investors, SRI advocates, and activist NGOs. This potent combination is effective in stimulating the raised standards in which all three groups of actors are interested. The Coalition for Environmentally Responsible Economies (CERES) and its work with the Institutional Investors on Climate Risk, or the Global Reporting Initiative (GRI) that encourages corporate sustainability reporting, demonstrate the growing convergence between SRI and pension fund corporate engagement. This form of co-operation was last seen in the 1980s during the South African anti-apartheid divestment campaign.

### Intersecting Interest. Past Campaigns: South African Divestment

The South African anti-apartheid campaign demonstrates one of the few early examples of convergence between pension fund engagement and SRI. As early as the 1960s, activists in the United States and Great Britain, appalled by political conditions of South African apartheid, began a massive divestment and boycott campaign aimed at abolishing South Africa's apartheid policies. The campaign's goals were to halt foreign trade and investment in South Africa. It had considerable public support, building on the success of radical activists who had opposed the Vietnam War (Becker and McVeigh 2001). "Public support for this campaign has been strong because South Africa's apartheid system of racial segregation and economic and political discrimination runs counter to the 'human rights' values espoused by the Western credo and because the black community in America identifies with the victims of apartheid" (Herman 1981, 273).

While the early anti-apartheid activists enjoyed public sympathy, the campaign, seen as moral in nature, had limited take-up by corporate interests in both the United Kingdom and the United States. It took another twenty years to build the institutional and corporate clout that would eventually bring down the apartheid system. In 1976, the book value of U.S. corporate investments in South Africa was $1.6 billion and U.S. bank loans were $2.2 billion. From 1960 to 1975, 350 U.S. corporations increased their investment in South Africa by 300 percent (Herman 1981). In 1977, thirteen minority shareholder resolutions were put to a vote in a campaign spearheaded by the Interfaith Center for Corporate Responsibility. Only three resolutions received the mandatory 3 percent vote to be eligible for resubmission the following year (Herman 1981). A U.S. Senate subcommittee reported in 1978 that the net effect of American investment has been to strengthen the economic and military self-sufficiency of South Africa's apartheid regime (Becker and McVeigh 2001). Yet by 1993, when calling for an end to economic sanctions, Nelson Mandela was asked if the divestment campaign had helped bring an end to the apartheid regime. "Oh there is no doubt," he replied (DeVilliers 1995, 197).

Even though the South African divestment campaign was morally motivated, it was able to bridge the gulf between traditional SRI and institutional investors' engagement (Smith 1990). As a result it was a much stronger force than the traditional SRI on its own. It combined public pressure, government action, and concerned individuals to establish the coalition between these two previously hostile forces.

Essentially there were two bridging mechanisms, one public and one private, encouraging institutional investors to adopt this moral position in their investment decision making. The first strategy was constructed in the public sphere and consisted of a multi-pronged approach, including consumer boycotts whose most prominent campaign was aimed at the UK's Barclays Bank. In addition, there was mounting public pressure for divestment within North American and British religious orders, charities, foundations, universities, and state legislatures. It was public rather than private pension funds that came under most public pressure for divestment during this period. By 1985, divestment resolutions were passed by several U.S. state legislatures and municipalities, among them Connecticut, Massachusetts, Michigan, and Nebraska, along with universities, including Harvard University, University of California, and Cornell University. While some university boards of trustees refused to adopt divestment resolutions on the grounds of fulfilling their fiduciary duty, many felt the immorality of apartheid required such action, particularly in the face of mounting public pressure (Dobris 1986; Simon et al. 1972).

Several state and municipal pension plans were required under law to divest from South Africa without regard to the impact of this decision on their portfolio returns. These public pension funds were challenged in the courts, but were found to be within their constitutional rights once mandated to undertake divestment from South Africa by state regulation, which in effect is their governing body.[4] Though many of the arguments raised in favor of South African divestment were moral in nature and despite prevailing views on trustees' fiduciary duty, profits were judged to be secondary to the method by which they were obtained.[5] What was required for moral arguments to prevail in these cases was a broad popular consensus on the immorality of profiting from an abhorrent, racist system. Prior to the South African anti-apartheid campaign no such broad moral agreement had emerged in the United Kingdom or the United States since World War II.

While U.S. public pension funds were found to be within their rights to divest from South Africa, private pension funds governed by the U.S. Department of Labor's Employee Retirement Income Security Act (ERISA) were not at liberty to incorporate such moral judgments into their portfolio decision making. With no superseding regulatory body, private funds were required to focus solely on the long-term financial interests of their beneficiaries (the duty of loyalty and the duty of care) without regard to the moral position being taken on South African investment. Yet private pension funds also took up South African divestment strategies. They provided the second bridge in forging the consensus between corporate engagement and traditional SRI. Private pension plans that took up divestment argued their case, not because of moral suasion, but rather from the position of protecting the long-term financial interests of their funds. In making their case, they pointed to the withdrawal of public pension funds from South Africa as evidence of political risk in the country and against which they needed to take certain actions to protect their fund.

From within the bastions of U.S. business, General Motors' private pension plan found an acceptable course of action addressing both the moral dilemma of South African investment and, more important, establishing a business plan for risk reduction in the face of apartheid. In the early 1970s, Reverend Leon Sullivan, an outside director of General Motors,[6] drew up a set of principles to be applied to General Motors and other firms operating in South Africa. At the time, General Motors was the largest U.S. employer of black South Africans. The Sullivan Principles incorporated a set of steps to reduce racial discrimination in the workplace through increased job opportunities, improved working conditions, and equalized pay. The Principles required South African firms to provide an annual report on their progress. Divestment from the firm was required as a last resort upon failure to integrate the South African work force into the ongoing operations of the company. Many private and public pension funds adopted the Sullivan Principles as the standard of behavior against which to make informed judgments on South African divestment. Failure to comply with these standards of workforce management were then judged to be risky behavior and as such was deemed negative to the long-term benefit of the company. Avoiding portfolio risk played a role in appropriate portfolio diversification and therefore met with the trustees' obligation to fulfill their fiduciary duty. However, it was not until 1998 that the U.S. Department of Labor issued an opinion letter confirming that private pension funds could indeed offer socially responsible investments under certain conditions.[7]

The South African divestment campaign marked a pivotal moment, aligning the moral rationale of traditional SRI with the new force of pension fund corporate engagement through a broad social consensus. In addition, it established an intersection of interest between an ethical standard of conduct by the firm and the reduction of risk for the investor. However, despite this success, it took another twenty years to align the interests of these two types of investors.

## New Divestment Campaigns

In 2000 we began to see an increase in divestment campaigns with coalitions of public pension funds, university endowments, and socially responsible investors. In most cases pension fund involvement in these campaigns has been at the behest of state and city legislatures that require divestment through government legislation. These divestment campaigns have included tobacco, companies doing business in Burma (Myanmar), and beginning in 2005 divestment of companies doing business in war-torn Sudan.

The Sudan divestment campaign is following a very similar model to that of South Africa. In 2004, the U.S. Senate and House of Representatives declared the atrocities in Darfur to be genocide. With on-going concern for the region and its people there has been a search for ways to condemn the activities of the Sudanese government during the civil war. It is acknowledged that divestment campaigns are effective in conveying a broad societal condemnation of such activity. By June 2007, eighteen U.S. state legislatures had called for their state pension funds to divest from companies doing business in Sudan including California, Colorado, Connecticut, Florida, Hawaii, Illinois, Indiana, Iowa, Kansas, Maine, Maryland, Massachusetts, Minnesota, New Jersey, New York, Oregon, Rhode Island, and Vermont.[8] Fourteen other U.S. States have legislation pending that would require pension fund divestment from Sudan (Sudan Divestment Task Force 2007). This campaign is part of a broader initiative that includes universities such as Harvard and socially responsible investment companies such as Trillium Assets. In addition, there are a number of rating agencies and analysts who are assisting these investors in identifying companies for divestment. One of the interesting differences between the current Sudan divestment campaign is that in most cases the pension funds are identifying the need to use corporate engagement with companies in order to bring about a change in their behavior before they would begin a process of divestment.

## Conclusion

Despite the convergence of traditional SRI and pension fund corporate engagement in the South African anti-apartheid campaign of the late 1970s and 1980s, traditional SRI and institutional investors maintained separate and quite distinct strategies for influencing and controlling corporate behavior. It was not until the late 1990s that SRI and corporate engagement once again joined forces in the struggle for corporate control.

The growing strength of traditional SRI provided investors with a powerful ownership position and granted them opportunities to engage with management on social, ethical, and environmental concerns. Simultaneously institutional investors, many of whom faced internal constituencies demanding greater consideration of social and environmental concerns, were recognizing the correlation between these objectives and profitable outcomes for the corporations in their portfolios. This growing convergence was further heightened by pension fund SRI disclosure legislation implemented in 2000 (United Kingdom 1999). The trend toward convergence was also notable in the United States where large institutional investors such as CalPERS declared the use of the Sullivan Principles that dominated the earlier South African campaign in their emerging market portfolios (CalPERS 2000).

The new alignment between traditional SRI and pension fund corporate engagement provides an interesting study in the struggle for corporate control. Most important, the two types of investors have a corresponding interest in the ESG aspects of firm behavior (these ESG factors are discussed in more detail in the next three chapters). As a result pension funds are increasingly building coalitions across the previous divide. The alliance between traditional SRI and pension fund corporate engagement offers a unique opportunity to advance environmental, social, and governance standards of corporate behavior. Whether that alliance holds or is fractured by the underlying contradictions between each group remains to be seen.

# 3.

# The Economic Inefficiency of Secrecy

No name is more closely associated with corporate governance campaigns than the California Public Employees Retirement System (CalPERS). With approximately $100 billion invested in public equity, CalPERS' interest in the governance and standards of the firms in which they invest is not surprising. CalPERS has long been an advocate of corporate governance and with a twenty-year track record, it has the evidence to back up its claim that well-governed companies outperform poorly governed ones over time (Anson et al. 2003). CalPERS has been so closely associated with this investment strategy that it has been dubbed the "CalPERS Effect" (Junkin and Toth 2006; Smith 1996).

In 1985, CalPERS and twenty other institutional investors formed the Council of Institutional Investors (CII) as a vehicle to advance their corporate governance concerns. During this period, the voting of proxies at annual shareholder meetings became an important tool for increased corporate control by these large institutional investors. Even without the U.S. Department of Labor's declaration that proxy voting is a plan asset, there was increasing interest by pension funds in using proxy voting as a tool for raising corporate governance standards.

There are two central aspects of pension funds' corporate governance concerns: transparency and accountability. Both are key corporate governance mechanisms used to control managerial behavior. These two concepts have become so inextricably linked in the current corporate governance rhetoric that it becomes difficult to distinguish them. But in reality, each of these two central tenets of corporate governance is derived from separate and distinct avenues of control.

While accountability involves formalizing the allocation of power in the firm reflected in the drive to increase board oversight of management through the enhanced role of independent directors, transparency is fundamentally about the availability of information to all the actors within the firm—principals, agents, and stakeholders. Pension funds use transparency to ensure that shareholders are the primary interest being served by the firm. Transparency not only aligns managers and owners, it also raises issues of firm behavior that allow other stakeholders to engage the corporation more broadly. Secrecy is economically inefficient. When organizations are opaque and interests are secret, decision making can and does distort efficiency.[1]

## Management and Shareholder Power

Displayed prominently on the walls of the CalPERS headquarters in Sacramento are numerous plaques inscribed with the mission statement of the organization:

> Our mission is to advance the financial and health security for all who participate in the System. We will fulfil this mission by creating and maintaining an environment that produces responsiveness to all those we serve.

Commenting on these plaques, former Board Chair Bill Crist said, "We put those up to remind the Board who it is we serve when we make decisions at CalPERS" (Crist 2003). Those whom boards serve and for what purpose are central to corporate governance.[2]

There are three major players within the corporate structure: managers, owners, and the boards of directors that mediate among them. In a perfect world all three groups work with common purpose. This idealized model ensures that all resources available to the corporation are put to their most efficient use and the resulting economic efficiency is deemed to benefit society as a whole. But with three sets of actors present in the modern corporation, the result is a separation of ownership from control (Berle and Means 1933). This separation results in agency costs within the firm that arise when managers serve their own interests rather than those of shareholders (Fama 1965).

Agency costs are by definition economically inefficient. Owners believe alignment of interests within the corporation is best achieved when all three groups focus on generating surplus profit from production and paying out that profit to shareholders in the form of increased dividends or rising share price. As early as 1919, the first U.S. court decision on the matter confirmed this view, declaring the corporation is "organized and carried on primarily for the profit of shareholders."[3] There is nothing in the action of CalPERS and other institutional investor owners that would disrupt this view. In fact, CalPERS' first Principle of Corporate Governance states, "Corporate governance practices should focus board attention on optimizing the company's operating performance and returns to shareowners" (CalPERS 2007).

Anglo-American common law countries rely on boards of directors to provide oversight for firm managers. These boards of directors are legally mandated to act solely in the interest of the firm. Nominally, boards represent shareholders, but they do so only indirectly by ensuring that management decisions add long-term value to the firm. Only management and boards themselves have the power of the proxy to nominate directors,[4] while owners retain the right to elect them. Given that the primary source of management oversight and accountability is the board of directors, managerial latitude is further exaggerated when chief executive officers hold the dual role of board chairmen, and "hand pick" the corporate director nominees to serve on company boards from their friends, families, and allies. Because directors so often owe their board seat to the firm's managers their loyalty can be divided.[5]

Owners' rights extend to the appointment of company auditors, as the quality of such reporting is crucial in understanding the material position of the firm. Owners exercise these rights at annual general meetings of the corporation, where they also have the right to place resolutions before the meeting and have those resolutions—as long as they adhere to a strict set of requirements—included in the company's proxy-voting circular. Since shareholders, particularly in widely held companies, usually do not attend annual general meetings, it is vitally important that shareholder-sponsored minority resolutions be included in proxy-voting circulars. However, in the United States these resolutions are generally non-binding on the company and even when passed, very few have been implemented to date. When fully described, the rights of shareholders, particularly minority shareholders, remain limited within the corporate structure, specifically when measured against the range of power available to management. The resulting reality is that in the past shareholders seldom exercised their rights, particularly given the prohibitive transaction costs involved in such initiatives.

Management extended its power within the corporation during the height of the takeover era of the 1970s and 1980s. Chief executive officers (CEOs) introduced staggered (or classified) boards, dual voting rights systems, and anti-takeover devices generally referred to as "poison pills." Early corporate governance campaigns tended to focus on such management driven entrenchment tools, resulting in an interesting alliance between corporate governance activists and corporate raiders—both of whom were determined to see poison pills and classified boards overturned, each for their own reasons.

The corporate governance movement and the role of owners were strengthened in the mid-1990s and early 2000s. First, the growing size of institutional investors generally and pension funds specifically (discussed in chapter 1) meant they had greater influence in equity markets. Second, the failure of corporate managers themselves to control excess within corporate structures was made evident by the failures of Enron, WorldCom, and many other corporations beginning in 2001. These failures meant significant losses for shareholders and resulted in regulatory changes, such as the U.S. Sarbanes-Oxley Act, and increased oversight by shareholders and by extension boards of directors who nominally represent them.

### Corporate Governance Mechanisms of Control

Transparency and accountability are the two primary corporate governance mechanisms used to control managerial behavior. But all too often, corporate scandals reveal that while formal structures of corporate accountability were in place, the interests being served in company decision making were secret. Justice Louis D. Brandeis observed in his aptly titled book *Other Peoples' Money*, "Sunlight is said to be the best of disinfectants, electric light the most efficient policeman" (1914, 62). While accountability formalizes the power structures within the firm, transparency provides both the sunlight and electric light needed to understand its activities. It could be said that accountability attempts to police management through rule-based regimes that assign power to each set of actors, but all too often secrecy erodes this carefully constructed edifice.

On the contrary, transparency makes clear the necessary information required by all actors to make appropriate decisions even when power distributions in the firm are unbalanced. While increased numbers of well-qualified independent directors is a necessary condition for improved corporate governance, it is not a sufficient condition without improved transparency. It may well be that the current over-reliance on independent directors as indicators of appropriate corporate governance will turn out to be misplaced if mandatory material disclosure across multiple aspects of firm behavior is not simultaneously required.

A clear example of the two corporate governance patterns can be found in the 2002 collapse of the corporate giant Enron. Accountability structures were in place at Enron, with independent directors composing over 50 percent of Enron's board. Indeed Enron passed a variety of corporate social responsibility screens and was included in several high profile socially responsible investment (SRI) indexes in the 1990s. Despite the presence of outside directors and other accountability mechanisms, it was unknown in whose interest directors and management served. In the three-year period leading up to the collapse of Enron, directors and senior management are reported to have sold $1.3 billion worth of stock. In this case there was too much reliance on independent directors to provide oversight in the face of too little transparency within the firm. Although Enron may be a case of larceny, it is a case of systemic larceny—one that can only be cured by increased corporate transparency.

What was evident in the governance failures of 2001 and 2002 was that the owners of these companies were not providing the active ownership required to monitor senior management behavior. Because managers in charge of day-to-day decision making will always have more information about the company, it is essential for information to be transparent to shareholders. In this way shareholders can hold management accountable and provide the external control necessary for efficient decision-making.

CalPERS and other activist institutional investors believe that firm-level transparency and shareholder value are inextricably linked. Table 3.1 offers insight into the characteristics these investors should look for in the firms in which they invest.

Long-term indexed investors need to push firms toward the upper left quadrant of the table, exhibiting both strong performance and high levels of transparency. However, all too often, institutional investors are willing to accept firms that fall into the upper right-hand quadrant of the table, with strong performance and low transparency (Enron would fall into this quadrant). Several other corporate scandals—including Hollinger International, Ahold, and Parmalat—should join Enron and WorldCom in the upper right quadrant due to strong short-term performance, lack of transparency, and loss of share value over time. While performance may be positive in the short term, investors in these companies face the risk that they will lose value over

**Table 3.1 Capital market transparency**

| Performance | Capital market transparency | |
|---|---|---|
| | High | Low |
| Positive | | Enron |
| Negative | | |

time because the actions of these firms are kept secret and the interests served may not be those of the shareholder.

The current acceptance of firms with high performance and low transparency is apparent when one realizes that, to date, no company with above benchmark performance has ever been targeted by CalPERS' annual corporate governance campaigns or focus lists. A review of other institutional shareholder initiatives finds few challenges to corporations with strong performance track records regardless of their levels of transparency. Hedge funds with annual growth rates in investment by pension funds of 170 percent from 2001 to 2006 is further evidence of pension funds' tendency to seek outperformance even when transparency is low. These funds, as with several private equity firms are notoriously opaque and yet, beyond challenging the fees they charge, there is limited information demanded of or given by these funds.[6]

It is companies located in the lower quadrants of table 3.1 that come under scrutiny in this investment framework. It is suggested that long-term investors such as CalPERS are increasingly willing to maintain their investment in firms in the lower left-hand quadrant where they exhibit below benchmark performance but with high levels of transparency, in the hope that over time strong performance will result. Ted White, former CalPERS' Director of Corporate Governance campaigns explained, "We need to see transparency. There may be short term performance downturns but if we see these things [transparency and good corporate governance] we are patient investors and wait" (White 2003). However, the quarterly performance benchmarking of investment portfolios and money managers' performance so prevalent in the pension fund world is on occasion at odds with this benevolent view of long-term ownership patterns. In reality, activist pension funds generally target firms in the lower right-hand quadrant of table 3.1. Here companies display both below benchmark performance and low transparency. It is from this quadrant that CalPERS selects companies for inclusion on its annual corporate governance campaigns.

Although corporate governance to date has been dominated by issues of accountability reflected in the drive to increase board oversight of management through the enhanced role of independent directors, future action should place more emphasis on mechanisms that force increased transparency and disclosure of the interests being served in firm-level decision making. In other words, there should be more corporate governance campaigns aimed at raising information within the firm than on creating structures to oversee managerial accountability. Pronouncements both from the OECD and from pension fund activists such as CalPERS demonstrated a nascent shift from accountability to transparency.[7] If fully realized, the result would indicate a shift in the axis of concern for pension fund investors from horizontal to vertical within the transparency/performance quadrants.

## Re-Emergence of Owners' Power

For most of the twentieth century, the Berle and Means' model described the corporate world of managerial power, particularly in Anglo-American financial markets. The wide dispersal of stock ownership beginning early in the twentieth century, combined with the advent of sophisticated liquid securities markets, meant that owners no longer dominated the corporate power structure as they had in the infamous robber baron era of the late nineteenth century. Corporate managers were deemed the major players. Owners, if dissatisfied with management behavior or low rates of return, were reduced to the "Wall Street Walk"[8] as their only available option.

The more dispersed ownership became through the mid-twentieth century, the more established the cult of the corporate manager became, particularly in Anglo-American capital markets. Managerial codes of conduct were inculcated within the corporation itself. The doctrine of the selfless manager was so prevalent that John Kenneth Galbraith described him as a manager who eschews the lovely and available women by whom he is intimately surrounded, in order to maximize the opportunities of other men whose existence he only knows through hearsay (1969, 117). These ethical codes were seen as coercion enough to ensure good conduct on the part of managers. Owners played no obvious role in establishing checks and balances to reign in managerial interest and power.

By the 1990s shareholders, particularly pension funds, began to use their influence through corporate governance campaigns in order to reassert the rights of owners in the corporate structure. To be effective this control mechanism requires a re-aggregation of previously dispersed ownership in order to bring real influence to bear on management decision making. Pension funds and other institutional investors with their ever-burgeoning asset base have come to control over 60 percent of all outstanding U.S. equity. More important than just their size is the investors' ability to act with a single voice on behalf of a multitude of beneficial owners. Essentially institutional investors are able to lower the transaction costs of monitoring managerial behavior that previously dispersed ownership made impossible.

This re-emergence of owners' power has been further strengthened by pension funds' newly found willingness to act in concert with corporate governance campaigns. The OECD Principles of Corporate Governance (2004) recognize the potential oversight capability afforded from coordinated action among institutional investors. But such coordination has not always been possible or desired. Prior to Securities and Exchange Commission (SEC) changes in 1992 these coalitions of investors were illegal in the United States. Even with legal changes, activist institutional investors resented "free riders" who benefit from the share price increases resulting from corporate governance campaigns, without bearing any of the costs.

After the 1992 SEC change in regulation, which allowed shareholder communication, the trend toward single campaigns has shifted. Organizations such as the CII started to facilitate increased direct communication between pension funds in order to promote meaningful co-operation and reinforce the ownership power each fund holds individually. Such coordination often takes the form of proxy-voting campaigns organized around specific minority shareholder resolutions.[9]

## CalPERS' Corporate Governance Campaigns

Beginning in the 1980s, CalPERS pioneered the use of corporate governance campaigns to influence underperforming, badly governed companies in their portfolio with the sole purpose of raising the share value of these companies for owners' benefit. It could be argued that CalPERS' early interest in corporate governance was driven by its enormous asset size—combined with the percentage of assets held in equities—specifically in the passive market indexes, which became increasingly popular in the 1980s and 1990s. Because of its size and breadth, CalPERS has been labeled a "universal owner"—one that effectively owns the entire market and therefore requires all aspects of the market to function as efficiently as possible (Hawley and Williams 2000). The result of these market pressures was to push CalPERS into corporate engagement with firms in its portfolio well ahead of other smaller pension funds that did not face similar market pressures until the technology stock market bust of 2000. It could be argued that of all CalPERS' attributes (defined benefit, public sector, trustee board, and location) its enormous size pushes it ahead of other pension funds in its activist stance.

As so often with early campaigns, CalPERS developed a negative tool to deliver its message. It created the "Focus List" of badly governed, underperforming companies, relying on reputational damage to accomplish its goals. What is interesting is that over time CalPERS' engagements have shifted from negative to positive, and have broadened in scope and scale.

CalPERS believes it fulfils its fiduciary duty to its pension plan members and beneficiaries when it exercises its legitimate right to raise the corporate governance standards of the firms in which it invests. This is because CalPERS and other institutional investors feel that corporate governance and long-term shareholder value are inextricably linked. They point to several studies that confirm the wealth creation impacts associated with what has become known as the "CalPERS effect" (Anson et al. 2003; Smith 1996).[10] One study performed by Wilshire Associates found that while ninety-five companies targeted by CalPERS between 1987 and 1999 had initially trailed the Standard and Poor's Index by 96 percent in the five years prior to CalPERS intervention, these stocks outperformed the index by 14 percent in the following five years. The value of this outperformance to CalPERS has been estimated at $150 million a year (Nesbitt 1994, 1995). Another study of the CalPERS effect (Anson et al. 2003) looked at ninety-five companies included in CalPERS' Focus List from 1987 to 2000. It found that prior to Focus List inclusion these companies underperformed their benchmark indexes by 96 percent in the previous five years. In the five years following their Focus List inclusion these same ninety-five companies outperformed their benchmarks by 15 percent (Anson et al. 2003). With its commitment to long-term active ownership,

CalPERS considers itself to be a shareowner rather than a shareholder and uses that terminology in its corporate governance campaigns.

*Developing Tools of Engagement*

Beginning in the late 1980s, CalPERS started to link good corporate governance structures with firms' long-term financial performance. With over 70 percent of their equity investments in passive index funds, CalPERS was often forced to hold positions in underperforming companies that were either poorly managed or poorly governed or both. Given that CalPERS could not sell these shares, they began to use their ownership position to force underperforming firms in their index funds to improve their corporate governance.

Corporate governance engagement in the late 1980s and early 1990s was more along the lines of a big stick than a quiet walk. Their annual Focus List of underperforming companies included a corresponding set of corporate governance prescriptions for each firm (see appendix tables A.1 and A.2). There was little discussion with targeted companies in the early days. CalPERS delivered its message via the media, utilizing the subsequent damage to corporate reputations as the lever to extract changes from management.

CalPERS was drawn into corporate governance in 1984 through their concern over the "greenmail" paid by Texaco to the Bass Brothers to avoid a hostile takeover. This fact combined with the formation of the CII in 1985 contributed to CalPERS' growing interest in the area. Beginning in 1987, their early Focus Lists largely centered on the elimination of anti-takeover devices that entrenched existing management within the corporate structure. Interestingly these early corporate governance campaigns forged an unlikely alliance between CalPERS and the notorious corporate raider T. Boone Pickens and the United Shareholders Association he promoted. Table A.2 demonstrates the early attention paid to anti-takeover devices as CalPERS's primary corporate governance concern. This type of minority shareholder resolution dominated CalPERS' corporate governance campaigns until 1990.

Beginning in 1990, CalPERS moved away from its preoccupation with management entrenchment through anti-takeover devices and added a new dimension to their corporate governance campaigns. They began to pay increased attention to the structure of the board itself, particularly to the role of independent directors. One could say that they became less preoccupied with the market for control (through takeovers of existing management) and more concerned with issues of accountability within existing management corporate structures. This shift is particularly noticeable both in the demands they made through the Focus List (see table A.1) and in the corporate governance statements, guidelines, and principles CalPERS developed throughout the 1990s.

*CalPERS' Focus List Campaigns*

Although CalPERS used its legitimate position as owners to engage and challenge managers in firm governance, its early Focus List campaigns relied more on threats to company reputation than on real shareholder power. It was reputational risk that forced companies to respond to CalPERS' demands.

Beginning in 1995, CalPERS initiated a more positive approach toward underperforming companies. They began to engage senior management in targeted underperforming firms through dialogue as their preferred strategy for corporate governance campaigns. "Our relationship with companies is getting better now. Over time we have become much more sophisticated. We are building analytic tools that support engagement on the business side. We let them know what improvements we would like to see in their governance structures. Only if we see no improvement do we include them in the Focus List" (White 2003). Even after a company's inclusion on the Focus List, CalPERS is prepared to withdraw its minority shareholder resolutions if management agrees to CalPERS' corporate governance demands.

During this shift to more positive engagement through the 1990s, CalPERS' corporate governance campaigns continued to be dominated by issues of accountability. At the forefront were CalPERS' demands for independent directors necessary to provide appropriate oversight of management. From 1990 to 2000, 42 percent of the fifty-seven shareholder resolutions put forward by CalPERS through their Focus List called for greater independent board and committee membership. Accountability concerns dominated CalPERS' 1998 U.S. Corporate Governance Principles and Guidelines and 2000 Global Corporate Governance Principles with independent directors' responsibilities to ensure the proper alignment of managers with owners.

CalPERS' Focus List itself draws on a sophisticated three-step process that narrows CalPERS' domestic holdings from a total universe of 1,600 firms to 300 firms and subsequently to approximately 10 firms that they place on the Focus List. Underperformance is the first test in the selection process with poorly performing stock measured by both market value and economic value.[11] Once a firm has been judged an underperformer, its governance structure is then scrutinized. Only firms with both poor performance and poor governance are candidates for CalPERS' Focus List.

Considering the corporate governance shift toward transparency detailed earlier in this chapter, in the future we should expect CalPERS to engage high-performing firms that lack transparency in dialogue aimed to improve their corporate governance and other standards. In 2005, CalPERS supported shareholder resolutions calling for increased environmental reporting at both Ford and General Motors. Ford responded positively to this engagement and produced the Ford Report on the Business Impact of Climate Change. In the spring of 2007 CalPERS withheld its support for ExxonMobil director Michael Boskin, when he refused to meet with shareowners on issues of climate change. It also supported increased disclosure on climate change issues by ExxonMobil, which has consistently refused to respond to shareowner demands for information and accountability in the past. Such actions demonstrate the demands activist pension fund investors are making for increased transparency from companies even when financial performance is high.

CalPERS' defines good corporate governance as mechanisms that create greater transparency in the corporation and greater accountability of senior management to their boards, and shareholders. In advancing these claims CalPERS clearly advocates a shareholder-dominated view of efficiency and corporate purpose.[12] This orientation is deeply routed in increasing share value as the primary purpose of the firm. CalPERS, in its drive to increase long-term share value for firm owners, often demands behavior from companies that would be described as socially responsible. In March 2006, CalPERS adopted an Environmental Corporate Governance Plan:

> CalPERs will identify companies in the transportation, utilities, and oil and natural gas sectors that fail to meet minimum standards of environmental data disclosure. The pension fund also will follow a new corporate governance guideline in acting on shareowner proposals for the timely, accurate reporting of environmental risks—especially those associated with climate change.

This new initiative is part of an Environmental Strategic Plan that the CalPERS Board of Administration adopted in 2005. But achieving more socially optimal outcomes is not CalPERS' central aim. In fact there are many within CalPERS who are uncomfortable with institutional investors taking on roles felt to belong legitimately in the public sphere. Rather it is their single-minded focus on long-term share value that allows CalPERS to serve both the interests of their own members and to use their market clout to raise firm-level standards.

In the aftermath of the Enron scandal, CalPERS' corporate governance campaigns increasingly focused on corporate transparency in its annual focus list campaigns. As Bill Crist explained in a 2003 interview, "Secrets are economically inefficient." Ironically CalPERS had been a major joint-partner with Enron on their off-book entities. According to the Associated Press, "In 1997, CalPERS, realized a $132.5 million profit on a $250 million investment in an Enron-led investment called Joint Energy Development Investments, or JEDI. That investment's success encouraged CalPERS to pour an additional $175.5 million into another Enron partnership, called JEDI II. CalPERS has received $171.7 million of that money back so far and eventually expects to break even on the deal" (2002). Responding to the inevitable questions regarding CalPERS' Enron off-book partnerships, senior board and executive members indicated that if they knew then what they know now, they would have made a different set of decisions regarding involvement with Enron. Public sector pension funds lost billions of dollars with the collapse of Enron. (The Florida Public Employees Retirement System alone lost over $335 million.) Transparent information would have helped Florida and many thousands of other investors make more economically efficient decisions as well.

The shift toward transparency concerns is notable in CalPERS' 2002 corporate governance initiative, *Financial Market Reform Principles: Returning to the Basics.* In contrast to CalPERS' 1998 *U.S. Corporate Governance Principles and Guidelines,* which primarily focuses on accountability issues, boards of directors, and particularly the role and definition of independent directors, this new document stresses transparency as its central theme.

The trend toward transparency can also be seen in organizational speeches and presentations and in CalPERS' 2003 Focus List engagements.[13] Of the nineteen requests made in 2000 to the nine corporations targeted through the Focus List, fifteen were concerned with board independence and one with transparency (see table A.1). In 2001 seventeen corporate governance requests were made to five companies; twelve dealt with board independence and four with transparency. This trend continued into 2002 when board independence accounted for fourteen recommendations and transparency for six recommendations.

By 2003, CalPERS' Focus List called for forty corporate governance improvements at six companies: fifteen (38 percent) called for greater corporate transparency, while twenty-one focused on board and committee independence (see table A.1).

This trend toward transparency demands in the Focus List declined in 2003. From 2004 to 2007, CalPERS placed a total of twenty-six underperforming firms on its annual Focus Lists. It identified eighty-three areas of concern and put forward nine shareholder resolutions. Only two items of concern directly addressed transparency issues and neither resulted in a shareholder resolution from CalPERS. In 2007, eleven companies were placed on the CalPERS Focus List. No items on the Focus list dealt with transparency issues (See table A.1 for CalPERS Focus List 2000–2007).

Rather than using the Focus List to advance increased corporate transparency CalPERS is using its presence in a number of global coalitions as vehicles to support increased corporate reporting, particularly on social and environmental issues. CalPERS' membership in the Carbon Disclosure Project and its support for the Principles for Responsible Investing demonstrate CalPERS' commitment to increased transparency. The shift toward transparency in firm decision making is critical as it makes information on firm behavior available not only to shareholders, but also to other stakeholders with an interest in firm behavior. For example, the Carbon Disclosure Project (CDP) provided a vehicle for CalPERS and its sister pension fund the California State Teachers Retirement System (CalSTRS) to issue a report on the compliance of oil and gas companies to CDP requests for disclosure on their carbon footprint (CalPERS 2006).

Currently most of CalPERS' transparency requests are general in nature, seeking a heightened role for shareholder and director exchanges of information rather than calling for specific financial and extra-financial material disclosures. We should expect that large U.S. institutional investors, including pension funds, will use this current period to test the effectiveness of the Sarbanes-Oxley Act's reporting requirements before calling for more specific transparency mechanisms from firms.

### Power Shift/Power Struggle

Shareholder-led corporate governance muscle flexing is already experiencing political backlash from both corporate management and the business media in Anglo-American financial markets. This trend is evident in 2007 with approximately 800 shareholder resolutions filed in the United States alone (ISS website 2007). Three hundred and fifty-nine of these resolutions addressed social or environmental issues. Little wonder these actions result in front-page headlines suggesting, "Battling for Corporate America: Who Will Come Out on Top in the Renewed Struggle between Shareholders and Managers?" (*Economist* 2006). It is believed that power never shifts without a struggle, and the managerial power of the twenty-first century is no exception.

Unlike other actors external to the firm, it is the legitimacy of this new shareholder power that makes it a significant force within today's corporations. But its very legitimacy is at the heart of the managerial backlash generated in its wake. Though shareholder rights strengthened during the twentieth century, particularly for minority owners in common law countries (LaPorta et al. 1999), it appears managers were only happy when these rights were not actually being used. Now that owners' rights are being exercised, managers correctly recognize that these tools represent a loss of power and control within the corporate structure.

In this power shift, proxy voting is seen as the major tool to restore shareholder oversight of managerial decision making. Witness the 2004 SEC decision to force mutual funds to engage in mandatory proxy voting and disclosure. Mandatory proxy voting is already required for U.S. pension funds under ERISA and such rules are contemplated in the United Kingdom under the 2002 Myners Report.

In contrast to some of the "big wins" by pension funds and other institutional investors since 2002, the early reputational attacks mounted by CalPERS and other shareholder activists in the late 1980s and early 1990s influenced corporate decision making with the threat of negative publicity generated by such attacks. Essentially, although early shareholder activists pushed for improved corporate governance in the name of owners, they acted more like outside agents than internal players. Firm managers could engage or ignore them at their will. CalPERS' officials acknowledge their early role as agents provocateurs rather than legitimate owners. Ted White explains in a 2003 interview, "Initially there was little or no discussion with the company before we put it on the Focus List. They blocked our requests to meet. This put CalPERS into the press as bullies. The Focus List was seen very negatively by companies." As pension funds began to use their ownership power through this period, company managers pushed back.

CalPERS' corporate governance campaign at American retail giant Sears provides an early example of this manager/owner tug of war. In 1990, CalPERS highlighted Sears' poor corporate governance and poor performance by placing it on its Focus List. At the time CalPERS held 2.2 million shares of Sears stock. "The message," said CalPERS then-CEO Dale Hanson: "From 1984 on, Sears went to hell in a handbag" (Monks 1994). In the previous year alone Sears had lost 15 percent of its value and much of the confidence of both analysts and investors. CalPERS, in an open letter to the Board, requested a separate shareholder advisory committee for Sears, agreeing to drop the shareholder resolution on condition that Sears management agreed to meet with CalPERS twice a year. During this same period, shareholder activist Robert Monks ran as an independent nominee for the Board of Directors at Sears, a move supported by CalPERS and other institutional investors. Sears management immediately launched a counterattack to prevent Monks from obtaining a seat on the board. Management spent $2.5 million, assigned thirty staff, and eliminated three board seats all in an effort to resist shareholder encroachment on managerial prerogative (Monks 1994). In this case Sears was successful in keeping shareholder activists at bay. Monks lost his bid to win a board seat, but radical changes did occur at Sears in the years following this shareholder challenge, changes that resulted in unlocking a billion dollars of shareholder value (Monks 1994).

In contrast to 1990, ten years on CalPERS's Focus List challenged corporate governance at Lone Star Steakhouse and helped tip the balance of power away from management toward shareholders. In this case CalPERS owned close to 400,000 shares of Lone Star valued at $7 a share, with a decline from $44 a share in 1996—a loss of $15 million. CalPERS' news release of the 2000 Focus List announced, "Lone Star Steak House finds its way on the list with some of the worst performance in the restaurant industry." Lone Star's stock had declined 55 percent over the previous five years against an increase of 7 percent by its peer group in the S&P Midcap Restaurants Index.

Analysts reacted quickly to rumors that CalPERS would place Lone Star on its 2000 Focus List. "It's pretty big," said Billy Haynes, a broker with Edward Jones. "When they put that list out, it is basically a list that all analysts and bankers will look at. It is like being blackballed from the party" (Memphis *Business Journal* 2000). Initially Lone Star responded well to CalPERS' engagement, offering three avenues of corporate governance reform: an annual CEO performance review, a compensation review, and a nominating committee comprised of independent directors. But shortly before the Focus List was released Lone Star closed off communications with CalPERS and declined to adopt other suggested corporate governance reforms. "Lone Star's insular attitude is indicative of the corporate governance weaknesses at the company that has contributed to the company's poor performance," said Charles P. Valdes, Chair of CalPERS Investment Committee (CalPERS 2000). CalPERS filed a shareholder proposal with Lone Star calling for the Board to have a majority of independent directors. This non-binding resolution passed with 64.5 percent of the vote.

At this same annual meeting there was an even more dramatic power shift within the corporation. Dissident activist Guy Adams—with the support of Institutional Shareholder Services (ISS; a proxy advisory company)—in a classic confrontation between majority and minority shareholders challenged and won the chairmanship of the board from Chairman, CEO, and largest shareholder Jamie Coulter. Though Adams, an untrained director with no restaurant experience, only remained on the board for six months, he successfully instituted a number of key corporate governance changes at Lone Star. In the year following the CalPERS intervention, Lone Star's stock more than doubled.

The struggle between owners and managers highlights the fact that while the market for control is nominally concerned with aligning interests, in reality it is about power.[14] At its core corporate governance remains deeply political; it is about the allocation of power, and therefore it is contested terrain.

### Evolution: Broadening Corporate Engagement— Relationship Investing

Firm-level decision making and power allocation are also the defining attributes of corporate engagement. What distinguishes corporate engagement is the scope of decision making and degree of power claimed in the name of owners. Given that both corporate governance campaigns and corporate engagement share a common lineage it is not surprising that when owners become active through the use of corporate governance campaigns, they often end up engaged on multiple levels with decision making and standard setting within the firms they hold in their portfolios.

This trend can be found across the world's largest DB pension plans.[15] The general pattern for these funds is initially to engage firms in their portfolio in a negative manner over strictly corporate governance issues. Usually the object of the negative corporate governance campaign is a significant underperforming, poorly governed holding in their portfolio that either for reasons of size of holdings or passive index lock-in, pension funds are not able to remove from their investments. No matter how trivial, the act of engaging as owners creates an organizational culture of active ownership within these pension fund investors. Over time these activist pension funds broaden their ownership engagement both in scope and scale, while simultaneously moving along the continuum from negative to positive engagement.

Examining the attributes of the pension funds that become activist owners, I suggest the trend toward such engagement is driven by pension funds' asset size, internal money management, and use of value-style investing techniques. Given that North American activist pension funds tend to be found only in the public sector, one might expect that the public accountability requirements of these funds makes them more sensitive to their role of providing enhanced market and corporate oversight. However, the activist UK private pension fund manager Hermes, with its ownership held by the giant British Telecom Pension Fund, refutes the assumption that all activist pension funds are found only within the public sphere. While the U.S. defined contribution pension fund TIAA-CREF has become a corporate governance activist, demonstrating that activism is not restricted only to defined benefit pension funds.[16]

The unifying characteristic across all activist funds is their belief that well governed firms outperform poorly governed ones, combined with their attitude that owners are able to unlock value through aligning principals and agents in long-term value creation. Given this perspective it is little wonder that activist pension funds use corporate governance campaigns to raise value across broad market indexed holdings (beta) and simultaneously use positive corporate engagement with a subset of firms in anticipation that such engagement will generate outperformance captured primarily within their own portfolio returns (alpha). CalPERS (and additionally Hermes and CPPIB and Ontario Teachers') call this aspect of their portfolio "relational investing."

Relational investing covers a wide aspect of firm decision making and marks a genuine power shift from company managers to owners with minority shareholders taking a greater role in both governance and day-to-day decision making in these firms. Companies selected for relational investing by these pension funds must view the involvement of the shareholders as a positive, agree to raise their corporate governance standards, and to have representatives of the pension funds—through their money managers—sit directly on their boards. CalPERS relies on external money managers with an expertise in relational investing to deliver this aspect of its corporate engagement. The largest of its external money managers in this corporate engagement arena is Relational Investors LLC that as of 2004 manages close to a billion dollars of CalPERS' assets on this basis.[17] The success of this program is not measured by improved corporate governance or any other broader social return, but rather by how well these funds have outperformed their peers.

## Conclusion

Pension funds are being increasingly called upon to provide owners' oversight of both boards of directors and managers of companies.[18] Such action represents a legitimate power shift within the corporate structure—one that is only possible given both the growing asset size of pension funds and their newfound willingness to act in broad coalition with each other. These two aspects of pension fund capitalism (Clark, 2000) lower the transaction costs of management oversight that previously dispersed ownership patterns made virtually impossible.

Within corporate governance broadly, two central themes dominate pension fund owners' corporate governance concerns, accountability and transparency. I contend that pension funds are increasingly shifting their attention away from accountability with its rules-based regimes aimed at formalizing the power relationships within the firm, and toward transparency that makes available firm-level information necessary to judge adequately in whose interest the firm is being run. While calls for more independent directors, separation of board chair from CEO, and executive compensation concerns will continue to be put forward by pension fund investors, increasing demands for greater financial and extra-financial material disclosure will be made. Secrecy is economically inefficient as it distorts the investment decision-making process. Transparency ensures appropriate investment decision making and simultaneously allows other stakeholders access to company information on which broadly to engage the firm.

CalPERS' corporate governance concerns shifted dramatically in 1990 from a preoccupation with anti-takeover devices to broader issues of managerial and board accountability. There has been a subsequent change in corporate governance demands in the period following the collapse of Enron and WorldCom. CalPERS' corporate governance demands are increasingly including requests for transparency. In 2007, the "Say-on-pay" campaign, seeking shareholder agreement on CEO future pay packages spearheaded by organized labor and public pension funds, garnered over 50 percent of votes at U.S. telecom Verizon. This marks the first time a shareholder resolution on CEO compensation has passed. It must be noted that U.S. mutual fund managers are increasingly voting against management on these issues.[19] This marks a historic moment for "activist owners" ability to demand greater management accountability and firm level transparency.

In light of the transparency pension fund investors demand, I anticipate a corresponding increase in disclosure by firms in order to attract and hold these investors. The increased use of sustainability reporting tools such as the Global Reporting Initiative and annual sustainability reports are witness to this trend. An indirect result of such disclosure will be greater access to information for a broad range of stakeholders. In the future we should find not only more efficient investment decisions as a result of increased firm transparency, but also more informed regulators, consumers, employees, and other interested parties. Finally, pension funds themselves, once providing oversight of firms, will become active owners, extending their involvement into other areas of firm-level decision making. The result is a further shift in the power balance between owners and managers and a deepening of the contested terrain of corporate decision making.

# 4.

# Why Do They Care?

Pension funds and other investors are increasingly sensitive to the impact of corporate reputations, which can add or destroy shareholder value over time, both at home and abroad. The result is that investors are demanding increased corporate social responsibility from the companies in which they invest. Because pension funds have liabilities that come from providing retirement benefits over long stretches of time, they face portfolio risks when substandard firm-level behavior leaves corporations open to reputational attack. Such investor vulnerability is no longer restricted to just the financial aspects of firms' behavior; it also includes social and environmental standards of behavior.

The world of pension fund investing is one of constant calculation of risk and return. In order to judge adequately the risk from investment, institutional investors increasingly demand greater financial and extra-financial disclosure from firms in their portfolios. Given the linkage among reputation, brand value, and share price, firm-level transparency provides institutional investors with the information necessary to make judgments about future corporate performance. It must be remembered that these institutional investors seek increased transparency without regard to the broader social obligations of the firm but rather as a means of protecting their investment over time.

Within financial markets, pension fund investors' legitimacy as the ultimate owners of firms makes their demands for increased transparency and greater corporate social responsibility more pressing than claims of outside agents within consumer markets. However, transparency in capital markets makes information on "poor" corporate behavior available to consumers and other key stakeholders. Increased information about the firm enables those inside and outside the firm to be more effective monitors of corporate behavior. In these cases, transparency can be a catalyst for attacks on brand image and may even prompt regulatory changes by those seeking to hold firms accountable to higher social and environmental standards.

The Carbon Disclosure Project, which represents $41 trillion of institutional investors' assets, is a good example of this concern for corporate social and environmental standards. It calls on companies around the world to disclose their greenhouse gas emissions and future reduction plans. Based on the information disclosed, these investors can better assess risk in their portfolios. But such disclosure not only informs investors; it also provides information to other key stakeholders including customers, consumers, activists, employees, and governments. As a result such disclosures have positive spillover effects for society at large.

## The Rise of Corporate Social Responsibility

Global corporations are closely scrutinized for their policies and practices across the world. How they treat workers in Indonesia, for example, can have significant repercussions for their reputations in their "home" markets of North America and Western Europe. Witness the public debate over global standards that affected companies such as Nike and Shell over the past decade.

There has long been academic interest in multinationals—their reach and responsibilities. Indeed, the development of multinational trading institutions like the East India Company and the Hudson Bay Company is a staple of economic history. What seems to be increasingly important is the accountability of global corporations to "home" markets even if nation-state regulation of their policies and practices across the world seems weak and inconsistent within the jurisdictions in which they operate. Often as long as companies respect "local" laws and regulations few governments are willing to challenge corporate policies and practices in far-off places. Given the dependence of less developed countries on foreign direct investment, "local" regulatory regimes are often lax and poorly policed.

Corporate social responsibility (CSR) is fast becoming an accepted practice for today's corporations. CSR practices dictate that companies value all stakeholders, customers, clients, employees, communities, and the environment, as well as shareholders. Under this rubric companies operate with higher standards than those demanded by law. Such corporate accountability may be less an issue of government policy and regulation (assuming laws and regulations are properly observed) and more an issue of consumer market and financial market pressure. Increasingly pension funds and other institutional investors provide such pressure on corporate behavior both at home and abroad.

The link between corporate reputations and long-term share value is increasingly evident for large institutional shareholders. It is this link that plays a fundamental role in why pension fund investors care about the standards and reputations of the firms in which they invest. Financial markets operate through the buying and selling of company equity. The price of a firm combines an assessment of the current value of the firm relative to reported earnings with expectations of increased or decreased "value" over the short and medium terms. Indeed, in the relatively efficient markets of the Anglo-American world where there is a great deal of information about the current circumstances of large-cap firms, future expectations may be the single most important element in determining stock market prices.

A good reputation signals to the financial market and analysts in particular that corporate "value" is likely to be preserved and enhanced. A good reputation is also a way of minimizing the intrusion of financial analysts and corporate governance specialists into matters of manager discretion while suggesting to the public at large that there is a consistent and mutually beneficial relationship between corporate managers' interests and shareholder value. By contrast, a poor reputation is usually associated with a sequence of "surprising" news of less than expected reported earnings, problems of business strategy, and perhaps poor corporate governance. Once established, a poor reputation invites greater scrutiny of managers' performance. Hollinger International's demise that ultimately led to criminal charges and conviction of its CEO Conrad Black shows that poor reputations also invite institutional investors to campaign actively in favor of internal "reforms" aimed at managers' compensation packages, and their roles and responsibilities.[1] Finally, a poor reputation may signal vulnerability in the market for corporate control.

There is a loose connection between corporate reputation and brand image. In many cases stock market reputation and brand image and management are directly linked through consumer sales. When corporate behavior anywhere along the supply chain runs counter to its compressed brand signal, the resulting loss of revenue is captured through changes in earnings. While a company's reputation can survive a single drop in reported earnings, it cannot maintain a good capital market reputation in the face of significant volatility in reported earnings over prolonged periods of time.

Outside agents, usually NGOs and other committed parties use the media as a form of involuntary corporate disclosure, releasing negative information designed to disrupt the desired brand images and corporate reputations companies wish to sustain. Such media campaigns often include direct attacks on the motives of senior company executives who can have a visceral reaction to seeing their names associated with corporate misdeeds and splashed across national newspapers. Attacks on brand image, combined with name and shame campaigns, have proven effective in delivering messages designed to disturb consumer loyalty and change corporate behavior. Outside agents attempt to provoke well-informed consumers into avoiding branded products made under substandard conditions with an aim of punishing corporate behavior in financial markets. A good example of such a successful campaign was the attack on Nike's reputation after it was learned that they were using sweatshop labor in the manufacture of their shoes and apparel. Beginning in 1997 an orchestrated consumer boycott of Nike focused on their retail outlet Nike Town was organized in the United States. Nike eventually responded to the demands to control the use of sweatshop and child labor in its supply chain in countries such as Vietnam and to allow third party observers to monitor its supply chain for these practices.

Nowhere was the clash of claims over brand and reputation more evident than the December 1999 riots aimed at disrupting the World Trade Organization conference in Seattle, Washington. Thousands of protestors took to the streets to disrupt the global meeting of trade ministers and other officials. Environmentalists joined forces with trade unions to protest the increasingly negative impact of globalization. Some may remember the "turtles and teamsters" moniker given to this coalition of concerned activists and NGOs. The protesters directed their anger at the storefronts of companies identified as part of the globalization problem. Newspapers around the world carried images of protestors attacking McDonald's golden arches, Nike's "swoosh," and Starbucks' coffeehouses. Protestors were able to successfully turn brand image against the very corporations who had created them and as a result inflicted reputational damage.

Corporations care about the impact of media attacks and consumer boycotts on companies' quarterly earnings statements. Damage to brand image can leap across consumer markets and into capital markets, influencing investor decisions and lowering share prices. It must be remembered that senior corporate managers are not only motivated by personal status and reputation halos that result from consistently high stock prices. In most cases their compensation packages are directly affected by the value of their stock options measured in current share prices. Even slight changes in consumer demand can affect investor and analyst expectations. Share prices measure expectations of future returns based on all available information; attacks on brand image and reputation bring new information to capital markets that may dampen future expectations. Hence corporate reputations and standards of behavior have become increasingly important to investors.

Considering the vulnerability of corporate earnings, and by extension share prices, to reputational attack, investors increasingly demand levels of transparency in corporate behavior and greater financial and extra-financial disclosure. Once transparency is in place, investors use their ownership position to demand higher firm-level standards of behavior as a means of protecting their investment from the negative impact of reputational attack. Increased corporate transparency is inextricably linked to value in both consumer and capital markets with direct consequences for the actors that dominate each domain.

## Institutional Investor Strategies

To illustrate the significance of reputational issues in capital markets, I draw on the experience of the Universities Superannuation Scheme (USS), one of the largest pension funds in the United Kingdom, and contrast its quiet approach to corporate engagement with that of the California Public Employees Retirement System (CalPERS). While both funds actively engage companies in their investment portfolios in order to raise environmental, social, and governance standards of behavior, each fund uses a different set of tactics in its engagement.

USS is a multi-employer defined benefit plan providing retirement benefits for nearly two hundred thousand current and retired UK university staff. It is considered to be a young plan with current active and contributing members far outweighing plan beneficiaries. USS faces long-term risk rather than short-term risk; it must be able to provide for its current members in the distant future. Consequently, the temporal structure of USS liabilities makes the plan sensitive to the long-term value of its holdings. With as much as 56 percent of assets in domestic equity markets and 23 percent of assets in international stocks, the precipitous decline of global financial markets in the aftermath of the TMT bubble hit the pension fund hard with its annual performance slipping below benchmark three years running. In 2002 the fund returned -16.7 percent with its asset base falling from £22 billion (2000) to £15.5 billion by late 2003 before recovering during the stock market rally of 2004. By 2007, USS total assets had rebounded to approximately £30 billion.

USS began its ambitious program of responsible investment in 2000 after considerable internal lobbying from a group of its members under the banner of "Ethics for USS."[2] A letter-writing campaign resulted in four thousand cards requesting ethical screening of investments delivered to the USS senior managers and Board members. The lobby group sought the outright removal of firms judged to be unethical from the USS investment portfolio on the assumption that this would, in some way, penalize firms by restricting access to capital.[3] USS senior management resisted the use of negative screens and instead opted for more positive engagement with companies in its portfolio. They took the unusual step of identifying climate change as the topic through which they would engage firms.[4] Broad as this agenda might appear, the top two holdings in the USS investment portfolio were British Petroleum (BP) and Shell Oil, accounting for £1.5 billion of the portfolio's £30 billion (as of June 2007). Considering the impending impact of the Kyoto Protocol on the entire sector, it is not surprising that these companies should be the target of USS engagement.

In 2001, USS released a report titled, *Climate Change: A Risk Management Challenge for Institutional Investors*, which opened with the following:

> Climate change is a major emerging risk management challenge for institutional investors. Institutional investors, and pension funds in particular, aim to provide pensions and other benefits through long-term investment. They can also be seen as 'universal investors' in that, due to their size, they commonly invest across the whole economy. If climate change threatens economic development, and especially if there are many or significant impacts, it will also therefore be likely to undermine the ability of pension funds and other institutional investors to fulfill their aims, so it is in their interests to see that risks associated with climate change are minimized. Whilst this responsibility is widely shared, institutional investors are uniquely suited to take particular actions. (Mansley and Dlugolecki 2001, 1)

Having identified climate change as its central focus, USS opted for positive engagement with companies rather than the perceived negative strategies of proxy-voting battles, minority shareholder resolutions at annual general meetings, and media-driven attacks on corporate reputations.[5] Because pension fund investors are driven by share price concerns, they use their ownership position to reduce the risk of adverse unexpected share price movements rather than as an instrument of social change. This kind of risk is increasingly understood in terms of the social and environmental performance of the firm, particularly when substandard performance in the third world sends reputation signals into the marketplace.

Despite USS' use of terms such as socially responsible investing (SRI) and responsible investing (RI) to describe their investment policy, this pension fund does not consider its actions to be part of the SRI movement. (For the vast majority of pension funds, the SRI movement is considered to be outside the mainstream of investment management.) Nor does USS align its corporate engagement approach with "noisy" pension fund activists such as CalPERS. While USS votes its proxies, it does not publicize lists of companies it plans to target for improvement nor has it ever submitted a minority shareholder resolution calling attention to firms' risky behavior. In fact, USS believes that these types of approaches are blunt tools that often fail to achieve the changes they seek to implement in corporate behavior.[6] From USS' point of view, the senior management of such targeted firms does not always understand the message that is being delivered by disgruntled shareholders in such forums. USS approaches its engagement with corporations primarily as a risk reduction strategy. By demanding more information and higher firm level standards of behavior, USS senior investment officer noted, "We are making capitalism more efficient" (Moon 2003).

In effect, USS seeks to pre-empt reputational damage before it occurs in consumer and capital markets, acting prior to a decline in earnings, share prices, and the price/earnings ratio. In this way, positive corporate engagement acts as an insurance policy taken out on something that does not occur. This tactic, however, can lack transparency, denying other stakeholders timely information on which to make decisions about the firm. In addition, the results are difficult to measure either directly through share prices changes or indirectly through corporate behavioral changes because of USS' behind-the-scenes approach.

Two examples of USS' intervention are UK construction company Balfour Beatty and UK pharmaceutical giant GlaxoSmithKline (GSK). In the case of Balfour Beatty, USS was one of many voices pressing the company to withdraw from the Turkish Ilisu Dam project. Late in 2001, Balfour Beatty reversed its position on this project and withdrew. Nowhere in the company's official press release is there a mention of institutional owners' intervention on this topic. But from anecdotal evidence, we know there was considerable behind-the-scenes pressure on the firm to avoid the negative reputation effects such an environmentally damaging project could inflict on its share prices.

In the GSK case, USS (whose GSK holdings are valued at £550 million) sought to avoid reputational damage and the resulting decline in long-term share value. USS urged GSK to withdraw from the court case against the South African Government for the manufacture of generic AIDS drugs. In April of 2001, GSK and other global drug manufactures agreed to drop their legal case and subsequently offered low-cost AIDS drugs to South Africa and other developing countries. During the same time, GSK announced profits of US$5.8 billion with only 2 percent of its revenue from markets in developing countries. Institutional investors believed that the potential for reputational damage from the South Africa court case far outweighed the threat posed to the pharmaceutical industries' intellectual property rights.

We can also assume—considering the size of USS holdings in BP and Shell—that positive engagement took place, it is hard to quantify its impacts given the magnitude of issues to be tackled. However, BP's pledge to move "beyond petroleum" may speak to the power of such institutional investors' corporate engagement, and certainly speaks to the positive reputational impacts of corporate social responsibility that more firms wish to associate with their brand. It must be noted that BP has come under attack for "green washing" its reputation. BP continues to generate most of its annual profits from traditional petroleum products and such events as the 2006 pipeline leak in Alaska have done much to tarnish its carefully constructed "green" reputation.

It is hard to quantify the effect of such leverage on share price and long-term performance. What is important is USS' pattern of positive engagement with firms that represent significant holdings in its portfolio on issues of reputational risk. Two of the three firms discussed—BP and GSK—are global leaders in their sectors, with strong brand recognition that could be easily tarnished by public dispute. Consumer boycotts in first-world markets are a real possibility given the sensitivity of educated consumers to these issues.

In contrast to the quiet diplomacy of USS, CalPERS takes a more direct, public, and sometimes confrontational approach with companies in order to offset reputational risk in its investment portfolio. It uses the threat of negative publicity to produce the desired changes in corporate behavior. With public disclosure integral in such engagement, the result can lead to greater transparency in both capital and consumer markets.

Beginning in the late 1980s, CalPERS began to use its ownership position in firms to raise standards of corporate governance. Arguably CalPERS' motivation in seeking higher corporate governance was the link between such standards and improved financial performance. CalPERS' officials indicated that becoming active owners fulfills its fiduciary duty to its plan members and beneficiaries. CalPERS targets poorly governed, underperforming firms in an annual "name-and-shame" campaign played out through the media. Because these firms underperform sectoral benchmarks, CalPERS assumes the negative reputational damage inflicted from inclusion in their annual Focus List will not further erode these companies' already discounted share prices. Here, the institutional investor acts as an outside agent threatening reputational damage if the firm does not respond to CalPERS' demands. Unlike during the early years of this campaign, CalPERS later started to provide for initial positive engagement with firms it targets but still uses the threat of reputational damage to induce company cooperation.

In 2001, CalPERS extended its corporate engagement to include broader social and environmental aspects of firm behavior. Following the 1998 Asian financial crisis, CalPERS' officials realized that its increased exposure to emerging markets left them vulnerable to higher levels of risk in its investment portfolio.

Most of the publicity on this policy decision focused on CalPERS' 2001 decisions to screen entire countries out of its portfolio (this decision and its subsequent change in 2007 are discussed in greater detail in the next chapter). In addition to country-level factors or principles, CalPERS also reports on individual companies in emerging markets on issues of broad corporate social responsibility including labor rights, human rights, and environmental standards (see table 4.1).

This company level screening has become even more critical as of 2007 with a decision to allow investment in companies that previously had been excluded from the permissible country list. In 2007 CalPERS eliminated its country–level screening policy and permitted investment in companies in all

---

**Table 4.1 CalPERS' company factors for consideration
in emerging market investing**

---

1. Transparency, including elements of a free press necessary for investors
2. Political stability
3. Progress towards the development of basic democratic institutions and principles
4. A strong and impartial legal system
5. Property and shareholder rights
6. Labor practices/harmful child labor
7. Corporate social responsibility
8. Compliance with the Global Sullivan Principles of Corporate Social Responsibility
9. Compliance with the International Labor Organization Declaration on Fundamental Principles and Rights at Work
10. Market regulation
11. Market volatility
12. Currency risk
13. Liquidity risk
14. Repatriation risk
15. Market openness to foreign investors
16. Government commitment to free market policies
17. Legal protection for foreign investors
18. Trading and settlement proficiency
19. Transaction costs

---

*Source:* CalPERS Investment Committee April 16, 2001

countries listed in the FTSE All Emerging Index. CalPERS' investment managers in emerging markets are subject to significant reporting requirements and must demonstrate how the companies in their portfolio lower the risks associated with emerging market investment. Not only does CalPERS apply these standards to investment decision making, it makes the result of its screening public, further increasing transparency and awareness of substandard corporate behavior. In its annual report on emerging market investments in May 2007 CalPERS managers indicated that fifty-three emerging market companies had been rejected from investment because they failed at least one of the geopolitical or investability factors in 2006. CalPERS uses its website to post these detailed company reports from their emerging market managers as part of their commitment to transparency on these issues.

As with the corporate governance Focus List, CalPERS is fully prepared to inflict reputational damage on these companies. CalPERS' deliberate decision to withhold investment in these companies leaves them unaffected by the subsequent drop in share value that may result from these reputational attacks.[7] Needless to say, when one of the world's largest institutional investors publicly withdraws from such investments the impact of the ensuing reputational damage is exacerbated by other investors' capital flight.[8] Such leverage across capital markets can have a direct impact on corporate decision making.

It must be noted, however, that unlike its corporate governance campaigns, which have both domestic and global reach, CalPERS restricts its social and environmental concerns to firms domiciled in emerging markets. These concerns do not currently extend to multinational enterprises in CalPERS' portfolio that face similar social and environmental risks in their global supply chains, or to CalPERS' domestic equity holdings. Given the growing threat reputational damage inflicts on share prices, it can be expected that the social and environmental aspects of firm behavior across all CalPERS' holdings will grow in importance. It seems likely that in firms in which CalPERS holds large positions, the pension fund will seek higher social and environmental standards through greater corporate transparency and disclosure rather than outright attacks on corporate reputation.

## Conclusion

Increasingly in this era of global markets and global supply chains the value firms place on brand image leaves them vulnerable to counter-claims about the virtues or otherwise of their corporate behavior. When corporate behavior runs counter to the societal norms embedded in their brands, outside agents may be able to target brand image in the media in order to highlight companies' irresponsible acts. Furthermore, the global supply chains characteristic to these firms leave them vulnerable to the very different standards of production between the less developed countries and the developed consumer markets of the West where the products are sold. Such media attacks can undercut the positive images these firms want associated with their products.

As a result pension funds and other institutional investors who dominate global capital markets are increasingly sensitive to reputational attacks on the firms they hold in their investment portfolios. The more extended the global supply chains of firms in their investment portfolios, the more reputational risk these types of investors face through their long-term investment strategies.

Because pension funds face increased levels of reputational risk in their portfolios, they are beginning to hold global companies accountable for their ESG behavior. These investors demand higher standards of corporate behavior than those required in many emerging markets, particularly in those developing countries where social, labor and environmental regulations are kept deliberately low to attract and keep these companies. In order to hold companies to account, institutional investors require greater corporate transparency and disclosure to judge adequately the reputational risks inherent in their business strategies. As a result we have entered a new phase in the relationship between large shareholders and their firms.

One consequence of institutional investors' interest in more detailed corporate information has been a growing market for third-party quantitative and qualitative assessments of firm governance practices. These types of assessments are a way of providing institutional investors the kind of summary information necessary for judging the risks associated with investing in different types of companies. Ratings firms publicize their assessments providing the market with systematic information on firms' governance characteristics. It is interesting to note that the ratings market has a variety of clients some of whom have a narrow interest in the form of corporate governance, whereas others have an interest in a wide variety of social and environmental standards. Indeed, there is an active research program among institutional investors seeking to evaluate the relationship between standards of corporate governance and social and environmental responsibility. If it can be shown that these two elements are related in any causal fashion then social activists may have a vital clue in their campaigns to affect the role and responsibilities of firms in global consumer markets (Bauer et al. 2002).

Finally I would suggest that regulators must sustain their current initiatives in the area of corporate governance—that is, improve transparency with respect to corporate decision making, ensure that boards of directors have independent shareholder and stakeholders representatives, improve corporate reporting standards, and expand reporting criteria so that the market for corporate ratings grows in ways consistent with the spread of information throughout securities markets.

# 5.

# Global Standards and Emerging Markets

According to Joseph Stiglitz, globalization is the "closer integration of the countries and peoples of the world which has been brought about by the enormous reduction of costs of transportation and communication, and the breaking down of artificial barriers to the flows of goods, services, capital, knowledge, and (to a lesser extent) people across borders" (2002, 9). While product and capital markets are increasingly globally organized, the legal and regulatory environments in which these markets transact are not. "[U]nfortunately, we have no world government, accountable to the people of every country, to oversee the globalization process in a fashion comparable to the way national governments guided the nationalization process. Instead, we have a system that might be called global governance without global government" (Stiglitz 2002, 21). Absent a single all-empowered global government the result is that most multinational firms operate in a tangled web of overlapping and sometimes contradictory regulatory and legal regimes (LaPorta et al. 1997, 1998, and 1999; Shleifer and Vishny 1997). Global firms take advantage of reduced corporate requirements in countries with lax legal and regulatory standards to lower production costs that otherwise higher standards would impose. This is particularly true in emerging markets where national governments often compete to attract foreign investment through lower standards. The resulting "race to the bottom" is for many symptomatic of globalization's failures.

In addition to the global production of goods and services we also find capital on the move. Here institutional investors, primarily pension funds, dominate global financial markets (Clark 2000, 2003; Davis and Steil 2001; Monks 2001). These investors are turning their attention to the world's emerging markets where rapidly expanding growth rates generate higher returns on investment than home markets can provide.[1] Anglo-American pensioners and future pensioners are increasingly dependent on the developing world's growth to secure the developed world's retirement living standards. By the end of 2006, the two hundred largest U.S. pension funds had invested close to $70 billion in these emerging markets (Pensions and Investments 2007). But conventional finance dictates that risk and return go hand in hand, and while the potential returns from these investments are high, the risks involved in such markets are equally high. The result is institutional investors' increasing vulnerability to firm-specific and country-level risks systemic to global capital market exposure (Crist 2003; Harrigan 2003; Moon 2003; Thamotheram 2003).

In order to access the information required to make sound investment decisions, pension funds and other large institutional investors are demanding systematic and standardized measurements of such extra-financial behavior (Hoffman 1996; Reich 1998; Rondinelli and Vastag 1996). The process of standardizing extra-financial information is not vastly different from the development of traditional financial accounting in the 1930s.[2] Such measurement, known as benchmarking in the pension industry, requires not just standardized and timely reporting mechanisms but also greater levels of transparency, both in terms of process and outcomes (UNEP 2002a). This phenomenon represents the global institutional investment value chain and this chapter maps its development. The value chain links the demands of institutional investors with increased unified global standards of corporate, social, and environmental behavior and the heightened transparency necessary to benchmark the outcomes of such behavior. What is interesting is that pension fund investors apply the global investment value chain not only to individual firms in emerging markets, but also to whole countries' corporate practices.

Nation states remain key actors in global standard setting. Countries and their regulatory regimes are central to external capital investment decisions. Convergence to global standards takes place when key actors in the investment value chain demand levels of corporate and social behavior greater than those currently consistent with countries' regulatory frameworks. I establish this claim using three critical pieces of analysis. First, I show that countries' legal origins are no longer strong determinants for achieving the global standards required for investment in emerging markets (for importance of legal origin see La Porta et al. 1997). Second, I demonstrate that emerging market countries, when facing foreign investment boycotts, improve their corporate practices and standards in order to attract that investment in the future. Third, I find that convergence to global standards is not strongly influenced by the wealth of the emerging market country, but rather is a direct reaction to exclusion from foreign investment in the previous period. To reach these conclusions I examine country-specific investment decisions made by institutional investors in emerging markets with particular reference to the California Public Employees Retirement System (CalPERS).

This chapter opens with the theoretical construct I call the global institutional investment value chain. I detail its significance in global standard setting and describe the agency claims I make for the key actors along the chain. Figure 5.1 illustrates the linkages and leverage points between actors, which I believe result in raised global standards and ultimately increased global equity and social justice outcomes. In the second section of the chapter I explore the attributes of key actors along the value chain and how such attributes contribute or inhibit action.

The third section of the chapter examines in more detail the extra-financial metrics used by actors within the chain to benchmark behavior. Here I interrogate the process by which certain best practice norms become global standards when demanded by external investors as a condition of investment. I seek to understand how convergence to these global standards occurs and which sets of actors and metrics are key in the process.

Finally, I test the validity of the hypothesis that institutional investors' demands result in country-level agency in global standard setting. I do this with specific reference to the Wilshire data set developed for CalPERS' emerging market screening during 2002 and 2003. The results have significant implications for conceptualizing the dynamic nature of the global standard-setting process. In contrast to theories of path dependency in global standard setting, I find that countries and their regulatory regimes are central to external capital investment decisions and that by using their investment leverage, pension funds can have a profound impact on the global standard-setting process. These findings deepen our understanding of the global institutional investment value chain and its function to raise standards of behavior and ultimately influence global equity and social justice outcomes.

## The Institutional Investment Value Chain

The global institutional investment value chain links the demands of institutional investors with increased unified global standards of environmental, social, and governance behavior and the heightened transparency necessary to benchmark the outcomes of such behavior (see figure 5.1).

Through most of the last century institutional investors only used financial metrics as indicators of current and future shareholder value. They compared investment opportunities across domestic firms that produced primarily in home markets. Pension funds benchmarked the financial performance of such investments using transparent reporting mechanisms that were both regulated and standardized. Most investment decisions were taken with only such metrics in mind. This investment approach worked reasonably well when most of the value of a company was tangible and therefore amenable to accepted measures. But toward the end of the twentieth century many companies underwent a dramatic shift in their balance sheets from tangible to intangible assets, including "goodwill." In the mid-1990s intangible assets composed over 50 percent of the value of firms such as Microsoft and Nike, much of that value associated with brand and reputation. One need only look at the loss of shareholder value from environmental scandals such as Exxon

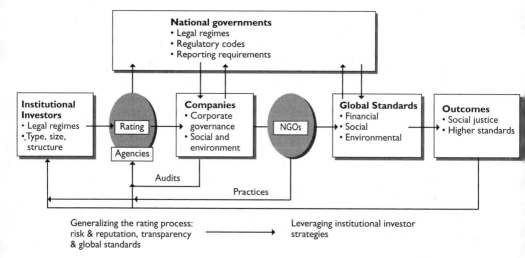

**Fig. 5.1  Global institutional investment value chain**

Valdez or Brent Spar to understand that investors now face reputation and environmental risks that were unrecognized fifty years ago (Graham and Dodd 1988).

For large institutional investors this unaccounted risk has been further compounded by increased exposure to international capital markets where firms operate under regimes with lax accounting systems and sub-standard social and environmental regulation. Given the long-term nature of these investments, it is little wonder pension funds are beginning to examine a variety of firm attributes to determine both future performance and degrees of risk in their investment decision making. But to access information on environmental, social, and governance behavior by which to judge the quality of investment, companies themselves must provide transparent and timely reporting. Given the international nature of institutional investment, their global reach requires not simply firm-level voluntary reporting but more stringent and enforceable national and global standards of corporate governance, social, and environmental transparency. Increasingly institutional investors, particularly in emerging markets, are judging national regulatory standards and legal regimes against global yardsticks to determine where to invest.

PricewaterhouseCoopers' Opacity Index (2001) and McKinsey's Global Corporate Governance Surveys back up such investor intuition that country-level corporate governance regimes, social, and environmental regulation— indeed entire legal systems—play a direct role in both potential investment performance and risk reduction strategies. PricewaterhouseCoopers focuses exclusively on country-level transparency in corporate governance, legal regimes, impact of corruption, regulatory practices, and economic policies and their impact on capital flight. McKinsey's Global Corporate Governance Survey and Emerging Market Opinion Survey establishes the equity premium investors are willing to pay for well-governed companies in emerging markets. Institutional investors indicate a willingness to pay up to 30 percent premium for well-run companies in regions such as Eastern Europe, Africa, and Asia (McKinsey 2002). Each of these studies points to the importance of country-wide corporate, social, and environmental regulation in investment decision making, particularly in emerging markets. Unlike domestic markets where investors benchmark firms individually against standard metrics, in emerging markets pension funds must rely on countrywide standards and reporting requirements from which to judge the quality and risk of their investment. Despite the fact that capital markets are now global, countries remain central actors in external capital investment decisions.

In essence, investors benchmark countries and companies against a set of global standards to ensure capital preservation and wealth enhancement in the face of increased country and corporate uncertainty endemic to emerging markets. Countries that fail to meet these standards face a direct and immediate loss of external capital investment (PricewaterhouseCoopers 2001). While pension funds provide the leverage for improved firm-level standards, nation states provide the muscle. Unlike voluntary corporate reporting mechanisms such as the Global Reporting Initiative (GRI), companies that do not comply with state regulation are in breach of law and subject to legal penalty. Surprisingly, while many companies balk at demands to raise their corporate, social, and environmental behavior, once implemented the results can be seen in rising profits, reduced costs, improved employee satisfaction and retention, consumer loyalty, and brand reputation—both in domestic and broadly international markets (Coffee 2002; Dowell et al. 2000; Porter 1995). BP's pledge to move beyond petroleum, Shell Oil's environmental programs, Rio Tinto's commitment to sustainable development, and Nike's oversight of supply chains that ensure compliance with company standards are all examples of international corporations with significant exposure in developing countries, which are actively raising their corporate, social, and environmental standards, and are reaping the benefits both in reputation and in share value.

In addition to investors, nation states, and companies, rating agencies and NGOs are also critical to the success of the global investment value chain (see figure 5.1). These agents provide the lens through which raised corporate governance and responsibility standards are both generated and monitored. Rating agencies monitor companies and countries, providing financial and extra-financial information from which pension funds and other institutional investors can make informed investment decisions. In contrast, NGOs and global standard-setting bodies are pivotal in establishing common behavioral frameworks and standards across multi-layered jurisdictions. Once these global standards are agreed on, such bodies become instrumental in pressuring firms and countries to adopt and meet these standards or face reputation-damaging consequences. These groups provide external monitoring of countrywide and firm-level standards using the media to make their findings public, in effect creating a venue for mandatory involuntary reporting.

## Pension Funds, Investors, and Global Standards

To understand more fully the dynamic agency of the key actors along the institutional investor value chain we need to explore the characteristics of these actors and their ability to raise global standards of behavior. Institutional actors are not homogenous or monolithic entities, but rather they embody a variety of models with characteristics that either drive or inhibit progress along the chain.

Within the set of institutional investors generally, we find a sub-set of pension funds and mutual funds (particularly mutual funds identified with socially responsible investing), imposing global standards of corporate, social, and environmental behavior on their investment decision making. For the purposes of this chapter I will limit myself to an examination of pension funds that engage companies and countries in this manner.

In essence, pension funds are capital pools administered by boards of trustees for the future benefit of plan beneficiaries. They can be either state-run schemes within national social security systems that are emerging in Europe, or private, employment-based plans common to Anglo-American countries that include the United States, the United Kingdom, Canada, and Australia. Most funded state security schemes are in their infancy and despite rapid growth, the bulk of pension fund assets continue to be held in private employer-based schemes in Anglo-American countries. The assets of these plans top $13 trillion and represent roughly half the investable assets in the global financial system (Clark 2000; Davis and Steil 2001; Monks 2001; Pensions and Investments 2003). These assets are found primarily in Anglo-American countries that share a common law regime of English origin, and a set of common regulatory codes and practices. In contrast, Japan and the Netherlands (two other countries with extensive private pension holdings) were developed under civil law codes; the former is German in origin and the latter is French. To date, pension funds in both these countries have had only limited practice using extra-financial benchmarking, leaving Anglo-American pension funds at the forefront of this new trend.

Interestingly both state-run and employment-based pension plans have engaged companies and countries within their investment portfolio in an effort to raise environmental, social, and governance standards.[3] It is defined benefit public pension funds, governed by boards of trustees, that are more likely to engage countries and companies within their investment portfolio based on their ESG behavior. The public nature of state funds and public-sector employee private funds makes them more likely to demand extra-financial standards in investment decision making than private corporate pension plans, which are neither subject to political lobbying nor want to invite scrutiny of their own corporate practices in return (Blackburn 2003).

Finally, pension funds can be classified by their asset size, investment style, and asset allocation decisions. Pension funds can choose to manage their assets internally or externally, actively or passively, and according to value or growth styles of investment. All these portfolio decisions affect whether funds will choose to participate in the global investment value chain. In addition, many funds have limited exposure to international debt and equity markets and often eschew emerging markets as too risky for their portfolios. Research shows that large, internally managed defined benefit public pension plans with active investment strategies, international portfolios and a value investment styles dominate the global institutional investment value chain.

Once the use of extra-financial investment criteria has been decided at the trustee board level, these public defined benefit pension plans turn to rating agencies for expertise in judging countries and companies based on both financial and extra-financial metrics. Contrary to popular perception, pension funds themselves have limited internal capacity to monitor the behavior of firms and countries in their investment portfolio. Moody's and Standard and Poor's remain the best known rating agencies, although neither one is strongly associated with rating extra-financial aspects of firm behavior. Following the Enron and WorldCom scandals, Moody's has added firm-level corporate governance to its rating services and we should expect to see increased recognition of the importance of corporate governance on firm performance going forward (Gompers et al. 2003).

Rating extra-financial aspects of firm behavior is currently performed by smaller boutique agencies such as Innovest, Kinder, Lydenberg and Domini (KLD), Coreratings, and Sustainable Asset Management (SAM). These boutique rating agencies use social audits to drill down into individual company's corporate social responsibility practices. In turn, these company ratings determine whether firms are included or excluded from large socially responsible indexes such as FTSE4Good, Dow Jones Sustainability Index, and the KLD Domini 400 Social Index. Many companies react to the reputational threat of exclusion from sustainable indexes as an inducement to both raise standards and provide greater transparency of corporate responsibility. Rating agencies rely primarily on already agreed sets of standards and codes by which to benchmark and rank the behavior of firms and countries alike.

In turn a plethora of non-governmental organizations, supranational bodies, and other global standard-setting bodies develop and monitor the global standards by which countries and companies are judged. These organizations run the gamut in terms of organizational structure, size, and reach, ranging from large supranational bodies—the Organization for Economic Cooperation and Development (OECD) or the International Labor Organization (ILO), to international agencies—the International Accounting Standards Board (IASB), the Coalition for Economically Responsible Economies (CERES), or International Organization for Standardization (ISO), to single issue locally-based networks—Oxfam or Friends of the Earth. These groups take responsibility for standard setting and subsequent monitoring across a broad range of corporate, social, and environmental behavior.

### The Global Standard-Setting Process

The mere presence of institutional actors in the value chain, regardless of their agency capability, does not fully capture how certain norms of best practice become global standards with wide acceptance and convergence. Institutional investors' demand for exogenous globally certified standards of corporate, social, and environmental behavior is a catalyst for companies and countries to adopt global standards or face capital flight.

Global standards are in essence uniform metrics used by institutional investors to judge the behavior of firms across regions, countries, and indeed international boundaries. They apply to corporate behavior ranging from financial accounting, executive decision making, environmental behavior, labor practices, and community relations. Codifying such measurement into global standards transforms individual corporate best practice into broadly based norms. Using such global standards not only allows for comparison across entities, but also raises the reporting transparency key to institutional investors' and other interested parties' decision-making process. Furthermore, widely acknowledged third party certification of such standards verifies their accuracy and provides a form of branding, reinforcing or repudiating the reputation of both the standard-setting body and the entities under scrutiny.

Global standards are usually initiated at the national level, often by actors directly concerned with the corporate practices to be scrutinized. These actors range from within corporations (e.g., the Nike labor practices code), across industries and sectors (e.g., the Mineral Extraction Code), among bodies charged with measuring industry behavior (e.g., IASB), or external stakeholders concerned with company or industry practice (e.g., CERES). Two elements are required in global standard setting: a set of measurement criteria and a certification process by which these standards are verified.

Due to the geographic reach of global standards, establishing such universal measurement criteria has proven difficult in the past. These metrics rely either on the strength and reputation of recognized international bodies such as the UN or OECD (see, for example, the OECD and its Guidelines for Multinational Enterprises or the GRI) or on third-party stakeholder groups who generate codes of conduct subsequently taken up more broadly (such as the Global Sullivan Principles[4] or the CERES Principles). Whether generated by internal bodies or external stakeholders, global standards provide uniform measurement allowing institutional investors to see inside the black box of firm production and to systematically judge the quality of investment.

This systematic judgment would be meaningless without the verification and certification of global standards provided by external agents. Pension fund investors rely on rating agencies to provide standardized information on countries' and firms' corporate and social governance structures and practices. In the 1990s and early 2000s the majority of information required by rating agencies had been strictly financial with dominant global players, such as Moody's and Standard and Poor's, setting standards for investment practice. However, increasing concern with extra-financial corporate and country behavior, particularly by institutional investors dealing outside their home markets, requires extra-financial global standards and the specialized rating needed to access information on these new global metrics.

Rating agencies in turn require countries and firms to provide timely and transparent reporting of financial and extra-financial material outcomes. In most cases the information flow on extra-financial metrics is voluntary between companies and countries on the one hand and standard-setting bodies and rating agencies on the other. The only government regulation in this area to date has been the UK legislation requiring pension funds to indicate via their Statements of Investment Principles whether they are using social, ethical, or environmental criteria in their investment selection.[5]

While there is increasing pressure to standardize sustainability reporting, given its voluntary nature these initiatives remain in their infancy (UNEP 2002b). The most successful effort to date in achieving extra-financial standardized reporting has been the GRI with one thousand organizations in sixty countries (2007). However, the GRI remains a cumbersome process, not easily accessible to organizations without specific expertise in the system. Other voluntary standardized reporting initiatives at the corporate level include the ISO 14000 environmental reporting series, the United Nations' Global Compact, AccountAbility 1000, and the OECD Guidelines for Multi-National Enterprises. These numerous voluntary reporting mechanisms make benchmarking individual corporate social and environmental behavior difficult and yet such benchmarks are required by pension funds and their consultants in order to make informed investment decisions.

In contrast to the voluntary nature of current firm-level sustainability reporting, the rating of countries' corporate, social, and environmental legal and regulatory regimes requires an examination of the mandatory, and some might say minimum, requirements imposed on all firms within the specific nation state (Reich 1998). Once gathered, this information is used to rate and rank countries according to the minimum financial and extra-financial aspects of firm behavior required under national law. This form of country-rating forces nation states to converge to global standards by comparing countywide outcomes and directly rewarding high scoring countries with external investment, while punishing low scoring countries through capital flight (for global legal convergence see Hansmann and Kraakman 2002; and Roe 2001). The result is a form of "yardstick" measurement by which to assess the quality of investment potential, particularly in countries that traditionally operate with low regulatory requirements and limited shareholder protection (McKinsey 2002; PricewaterhouseCoopers 2001; Shleifer 1985).

The type of country-level information sought by rating agencies on behalf of pension funds includes broad sociopolitical aspects such as degrees of transparency, political stability, and productive labor practices. Critical capital market practices such as liquidity, regulation, investor protection, accounting standards, capital market openness, settlement proficiency, and transaction costs are also rated and ranked. In order to compare and adequately benchmark these statistics across countries, rating agencies rely on global standards against which to judge the behavior of individual states.

Universal metrics tend to follow a pattern beginning as best practice adopted voluntarily across nations, and gradually becoming an accepted norm of behavior. International accounting standards for example, extended the Generally Accepted Accounting Principles (GAAP) of nine countries (Australia, Canada, France, Germany, Japan, Mexico, the Netherlands, the United

Kingdom and Ireland, and the United States) into a unified code, thus creating the IAS global standard increasingly adopted across multiple jurisdictions (Financial Times 2003). Institutional investors, especially following the Asian financial crisis of 1998, often demand that IAS standards are met before they invest. Such external demand forces countries to meet this norm. These external investor demands are particularly prevalent in countries with weak legal frameworks and a lack of shareholder protection, further accelerating convergence to a global norm.

This same pattern has been repeated across other areas of corporate and national behavior over the past thirty years. The Global Sullivan Principles, the CERES Environmental Principles, ILO Core Labor Standards, OECD Guidelines for Multi-National Enterprises are all examples of voluntary codes of behavior developed by non-governmental bodies, and demanded by institutional investors as a condition of investment. Much as we see with accounting principles, countries' legal and regulatory regimes begin to converge to these social standards when they are backed up by potential loss of external capital investment.

Fundamentally global standards remain voluntary, and without subsequent national adoption into legal and regulatory frameworks they are unenforceable in today's global governance environment. Arguably when institutional investors engage in the global investment value chain they bring pressure that translates global standards into the required national laws and regulations, resulting in such standards becoming binding on all firms whether they are local producers, sub-contractors or, multi-national enterprises (Hoffman 1996; Rondinelli and Vastag 1996).

## CalPERS' Emerging Markets Policy

The global investment value chain provides a useful construct for understanding institutional investors' ability to raise global standards of corporate, social, and environmental behavior. It suggests that countries and their regulatory regimes remain key to external capital market decisions, particularly in areas of high risk such as we find in emerging markets. Having developed this theoretical framework I now test its validity against CalPERS' actual investment decisions.

In February 2002, CalPERS stunned the financial world with their decision to remove entire countries from their emerging markets portfolio based on country-specific factors, including political stability, transparency; and productive labor practices combined with capital market factors of liquidity and volatility, regulation, openness, settlement proficiency, and transaction costs. CalPERS, then the largest pension fund in the world, stated that such a move lowered risk in emerging markets and therefore fulfilled its fiduciary obligations to both pension plan beneficiaries and plan sponsors. While CalPERS had a previous history of declared non-investable emerging markets, their decision marked the first time that such a list was based on both financial and extra-financial criteria. The world's business media was stunned by such a bold and sweeping decision on the part of a major global investor, a decision that effectively removed 25 percent of the available emerging market investment from CalPERS' portfolio.

Traditional financial analysts argued that such blanket screening, particularly based on extra-financial criteria, compromised CalPERS' potential portfolio returns because it neither gains from investing in the full market (beta), nor allows for the possibility of finding market outperformance (alpha) in countries systematically removed from the portfolio. Based on this analysis such an investment decision automatically underperforms more complete emerging market indexes and benchmarks. Interestingly, CalPERS' emerging markets decision also drew criticism from development NGOs on the grounds that countrywide exclusionary screens act as barriers to the overall development needed by these countries in order to raise living standards. Not only did CalPERS' officials have to brave the condemnation of both traditional financial analysts and NGOs they also faced the Philippines Government's instant rebuttal of their data, and three months later CalPERS reinstated the Philippines in their investment portfolio. Given the levels of internal debate within CalPERS on the advisability of using countrywide screens, capped off with a narrow seven-to-six Board vote in its favor, it was not an auspicious start for this bold initiative. Nor is it surprising that by 2007, when it was determined that the emerging markets screened portfolio had underperformed its benchmark by 2.6 percent, CalPERS board made the decision to allow its emerging markets managers to invest in individual companies subject to strict reporting criteria, in all countries listed in the FTSE All Emerging Index.

CalPERS shifted the onus of investment decision making in these markets to its emerging market managers. Its original seven county specific investment factors developed in 2001 have been replaced with eight emerging market principles (see table 5.1)

---

### Table 5.1 CalPERS emerging market principles

---

1. Political stability and the development of basic democratic institutions and principles
2. Transparency of information, including the elements of a free press
3. No harmful labor practices or use of child labor; compliance with the International Labor Organization Declaration on the Fundamental Principles and Rights at Work
4. Corporate social responsibility and compliance with the Global Sullivan Principles of Corporate Social Responsibility
5. Adequate market regulation and liquidity
6. Commitment to free market policies and openness to foreign investors
7. Reasonable trading and settlement proficiency and reasonable transaction costs
8. Appropriate disclosure on environmental, social, and corporate governance issues

---

*Source:* CalPERS Permissible Equity Markets Policy, Investment Committee, August 13, 2007

---

Emerging market managers are required to report annually to the CalPERS Investment committee on how they are taking the principles into account in their investment decisions, including a list of data sources used to evaluate the principles in the countries where they invested. It remains to be seen what impact this change will have on countries (e.g., China) formerly excluded from CalPERS permissible markets list.

In 2002, after a lengthy consultation process, CalPERS chose to maintain investment in thirteen of the twenty-seven countries within the emerging market investment universe.[6] These countries included Argentina, Brazil, Chile, Czech Republic, Hungary, Israel, Mexico, Peru, Poland, South Africa, South Korea, Taiwan, and Turkey (with the Philippines reinstated in May 2002). All countries included for investment had Wilshire scores of 2.00 or higher.[7] Excluded from investment were China, Colombia, Egypt, India, Indonesia, Jordan, Malaysia, Morocco, Pakistan, Russia, Sri Lanka, and Thailand. The impact of exclusion from CalPERS' portfolio went well beyond CalPERS' own direct investment. The reputational damage caused a domino effect with other foreign investors divesting from these countries. Even the three-month exclusion of the Philippines resulted in millions of dollars of external capital flight for that country (Harber 2003).

Although many financial analysts argue that investment decisions should only be made based on examination of individual companies' behavior, the global investment value chain posits that in the absence of global government nation states remain key actors in global standard setting (Crist 2003; Harrigan 2003). Countries and their regulatory regimes are central to external capital investment decisions. Convergence to global standards occurs when key actors in the investment value chain demand levels of corporate and social behavior greater than those currently consistent with countries' own regulatory frameworks. Such demands force countries to establish global standards as country norms of behavior in order to attract and hold external investment. I use CalPERS' emerging markets screening data over two years (2002 and 2003) to test this hypothesis.

## Significance of Legal Origin and Convergence to Global Standards

Factors that lie behind capital market decision making have long been the subject of academic work in finance, economics, and economic geography. La Porta and colleagues (1997) argue that external capital investment decisions are deeply influenced by the origins of countries' legal regimes. They analyzed external capital flows of forty-nine countries based on their legal origin. Their findings showed that minority shareholder rights deeply entrenched in English origin common law countries attract and sustain greater external capital investment, resulting in deeper capital markets than civil code countries of French, German, and Scandinavian origin. This chapter raises the question of whether the path dependence of legal origin described by La Porta and his colleagues' hypothesis holds for today's emerging markets and their ability to attract and hold external finance (for in depth analysis of path dependency see, for example, Arthur 1992; Grabher 1993). Differing from the approach taken by La Porta and his colleagues, I argue that while past legal regimes may have had some initial influence on determining levels of external investment and capital market development, countries are no longer chained to their past but rather are active agents that shape their future through convergence to global capital market standards. The speed by which countries regulate such capital market convergence is the mechanism that attracts and holds today's global investors. Countries' ability and willingness to adopt these standards in the face of capital market exclusion is unrelated to the origins of their legal regimes.

Using Wilshire 2002 and 2003 data on the seven country and market factors and twenty-two sub-factors that determined CalPERS' investment across twenty-seven emerging market countries (see table 5.2), I tested the La Porta hypothesis to see if legal origin played a role in determining CalPERS' emerging market investment decision making. I used three legal regime families: English, French, and German[8] and examined their mean Wilshire scores. First, I found the German family to have mean total Wilshire score significantly higher than the other families in both 2002 and 2003. Second, while in 2002 the French family significantly outscored the English one, in 2003 the situation reversed with the English origin family scoring second. Significant differences between the families of legal origin also exist at the level of sub-factors of the Wilshire scores. However, the question remains whether these rankings are really determined by the legal origin of the countries involved. Table 5.2 shows that countries representing the German family are some of the wealthiest economies in the sample. In fact, the correlation coefficient between a country's GDP per capita[9] and its total Wilshire score was as high as 0.76.

In order to account for the level of income while investigating the relationship between the Wilshire scores and the families of legal origin, I regressed countries' Wilshire scores (for all twenty-seven countries) on the GDP per capita as well as the dummy variables of legal origin. The income level proved significant for total scores (at 1 percent confidence level), as well as scores on labor practices, and political stability. In contrast, the inclusion of a country in one or another family of legal origin did not bear any significance for the country's Wilshire rating, the total score, or the score in any of the sub-factors.

With strong correlation between GDP per capita and Wilshire scores one might conclude that countries' initial endowments play the central role in determining future external investment, thus perpetuating the path-dependent nature of development.[10] But the dynamic data tell a very different story: one of active agents converging quickly to global standards in order to attract CalPERS' future investment. Between 2002, when CalPERS began emerging market country screening based on these factors, and 2003, the average score for all twenty-seven countries in the survey increased dramatically rising 10 basis points from 1.89 to 1.98 over one year. In nineteen countries, scores increased with large improvements for many of the poorest emerging market countries. Morocco, Malaysia, Sri Lanka, and Jordan topped the list for country and market factor improvements over the year. All four countries had been excluded from CalPERS' investment the previous year. Jordan's score increase, rising from 1.74 to 2.10 resulted in inclusion in CalPERS' 2003 emerging market investment portfolio.

In eight countries with declining scores (seven of which had been included in the 2002 emerging market portfolio) the greatest deterioration over the year was in the areas of transaction costs and political stability (see table 5.3). Within the transparency factor the sub-factors that deteriorated most were accounting standards as well as monetary and fiscal transparency. The meeting between CalPERS' officials and members of the Brazilian government in March 2003 evidenced the seriousness with which these countries take CalPERS' annual ratings. The Brazilian government—alarmed to find itself on the threshold level of CalPERS' ratings at 2.00—specifically requested CalPERS' Board Chair Sean Harrigan come to Brazil in an effort to improve the Brazilian standards necessary to raise its score in 2004 (Harrigan 2003; Pensions and Investments 2003).

In the ten sample countries where scores improved by at least 0.20 the most important factors were positive increases in regulation with improvements in creditors' and shareholders' rights, and transaction costs (see table 5.4). We can see that with the exception of transaction costs, the factors behind the improvement in country scores differed considerably from those factors behind others' decline. Transaction costs appear to be a dynamic characteristic of emerging markets, often driven by capital markets themselves and therefore exogenous to country control. However, improvements in regulation and transparency improvements are clearly within each countries' control, and both had high degrees of changeability in the twenty-seven emerging markets examined. The stability and changeability of scores can be measured by the total of the absolute value of change in the score for each country (see table 5.5). Across the seven country and market factors used in the analysis, we see limited change in capital market openness and no change in productive labor standards. The lack of improvement in productive labor practices is notable given the sentiment by critics of CalPERS' emerging market country screening that it was a policy decision driven by trade union influence on the CalPERS' Board of Directors. A closer examination of the four labor sub-factors that generate the total Wilshire labor score reveals a positive increase in productive labor practices across thirteen emerging markets, with Venezuela achieving the highest positive change in this category over the year. On the contrary, thirteen countries registered declining labor practices with India's standards falling the most. However, all of these changes

## Table 5.2 Wilshire total scores

| 2003 legal regime | origin | Wilshire 2003 | Wilshire score 2003/02 comparison 2003 | 2002 | Difference |
|---|---|---|---|---|---|
| South Korea | German | 2.75 | 2.80 | 2.55 | 0.25 |
| Poland | Russian/German | 2.56 | 2.48 | 2.39 | 0.09 |
| Israel | English | 2.55 | 2.52 | 2.36 | 0.16 |
| Czech Republic | German | 2.50 | 2.45 | 2.25 | 0.20 |
| Hungary | Customary | 2.50 | 2.45 | 2.50 | -0.05 |
| Taiwan | German | 2.42 | 2.47 | 2.52 | -0.05 |
| South Africa | English | 2.33 | 2.38 | 2.17 | 0.21 |
| Chile | French | 2.31 | 2.38 | 2.44 | -0.06 |
| Mexico | French | 2.25 | 2.25 | 2.10 | 0.15 |
| Jordan | French | 2.13 | 2.10 | 1.74 | 0.36 |
| Peru | French | 2.12 | 2.09 | 2.21 | −0.12 |
| Argentina | French | 2.09 | 2.09 | 2.63 | −0.54 |
| Turkey | French | 2.08 | 2.03 | 2.02 | 0.01 |
| Brazil | French | 2.00 | 2.05 | 2.10 | −0.05 |
| India | English | 1.92 | 1.97 | 1.73 | 0.24 |
| Malaysia | English | 1.80 | 1.87 | 1.45 | 0.42 |
| Morocco | French | 1.80 | 1.82 | 1.25 | 0.57 |
| Sri Lanka | English | 1.74 | 1.74 | 1.31 | 0.43 |
| Thailand | English | 1.72 | 1.79 | 1.64 | 0.15 |
| Colombia | French | 1.67 | 1.67 | 1.42 | 0.25 |
| China | Chinese/Confucian | 1.50 | 1.55 | 1.45 | 0.10 |
| Egypt | French | 1.50 | 1.45 | 1.58 | −0.13 |
| Pakistan | English | 1.50 | 1.55 | 1.40 | 0.15 |
| Philippines | French | 1.46 | 1.53 | 2.06 | −0.53 |
| Russia | Russian | 1.38 | 1.35 | 1.15 | 0.20 |
| Venezuela | French | 1.30 | 1.32 | 1.32 | 0.00 |
| Indonesia | French | 1.25 | 1.35 | 1.25 | 0.10 |

Source: Wilshire 2003 with legal regimes from Reynolds and Flores (1993).

* The Wilshire 2003 total score was used to determine CalPERS' emerging markets investment portfolio. All countries with scores of 2.0 and higher were included for investment, with the exception
of the Philippines where data issues remain. The 2003 total score differs from the 2003/2002 comparison score due to weightings used in 2002. In order to compare accurately Wilshire used the
2002 weightings for this part of the analysis.

## Table 5.3 Comparison of countries with decreased scores* (2002/2003)

| | Political stability | Transparency | Labor | Market liquidity | Regulation | Capital market | Settlement | Transaction costs |
|---|---|---|---|---|---|---|---|---|
| Argentina | −1 | −2 | | | | | | −1 |
| Brazil | | | | −1 | | | −1 | −1 |
| Chile | | −1 | | | | | +1 | |
| Egypt | −1 | −1 | | +1 | | | +1 | |
| Hungary | | | | −1 | +1 | | | −2 |
| Peru | −1 | | | | | | +1 | −1 |
| Philippines | −1 | −1 | | | −1 | | +2 | −1 |
| Taiwan | | | | | | | | −1 |

*Source:* Authors' calculations based on Wilshire 2003.

CalPERS' seven country and market factors are scored on a rating scale of 1 to 3, with 3 being the highest possible rating and therefore highest standards achieved. Tables 5.3 and 5.4 indicate areas where countries gained or lost points in their ratings in a comparison of their 2002 and 2003 scores.

## Table 5.4 Comparison of countries with increased scores of .20 or better (2002/2003)

| | Political stability | Transparency | Labor | Market liquidity | Regulation | Capital market | Settlement | Transaction costs |
|---|---|---|---|---|---|---|---|---|
| Colombia | | | | | +1 | | | +1 |
| Czech R. | | | | | | | | +2 |
| India | | −1 | | | | | | +2 |
| Jordan | | +1 | | +1 | +1 | +1 | | −1 |
| Malaysia | +1 | | | +1 | +1 | | | +1 |
| Morocco | +1 | | | | +1 | | | +2 |
| Russia | | | | | +1 | | | |
| S. Africa | | +1 | | +1 | | | | |
| S. Korea | | | | | +2 | | | |
| Sri Lanka | +1 | +1 | | | +1 | | | |

*Source:* Authors' calculations based on Wilshire 2003.

**Table 5.5 Stability and changeability of scores:**
**Absolute value of full sample change (2002/2003)\***

| | Political stability | Transparency | Labor | Market liquidity | Regulation | Capital market | Settlement | Transaction costs |
|---|---|---|---|---|---|---|---|---|
| Change | 7 | 12 | 0 | 7 | 17 | 2 | 17 | 19 |

*Source:* Authors' calculations based on Wilshire 2003.

*Note each factor was given equal weighting in determining Total Wilshire score. Wilshire total and sub-scores were regressed on the level of GDP per capita in 2002 and the dummy variables representing the family of legal origin (with legal origin other than English, French, or German treated as a reference category). The resulting standardized regression coefficients (in columns) for each Wilshire total or sub-score (in rows) as well as the coefficients of determination (adjusted R2) are presented in the following table. Number of cases in each regression equals 27, representing the number of countries rated by Wilshire.

| Wilshire score or sub-score used as dependent variable | Standardized regression coefficients and their significance | | | | | |
|---|---|---|---|---|---|---|
| | | | Family of legal origin | | | Adjusted |
| | GDP | | English | French | German | R2 |
| Total 2003 | 0.70 | *** | 0.23 | 0.26 | 0.30 | 0.55 |
| Total 2002 | 0.73 | *** | 0.11 | 0.38 | 0.20 | 0.56 |
| Political stability | 0.37 | *** | 0.15 | −0.03 | 0.44 | 0.45 |
| Transparency | 0.40 | | 0.07 | 0.04 | 0.07 | 0.03 |
| Labor | 0.79 | *** | 0.12 | 0.39 | 0.11 | 0.47 |
| Market liquidity | 0.01 | | -0.24 | −0.37 | 0.06 | 0.03 |
| Regulation | 0.56 | * | 0.42 | 0.11 | -0.14 | 0.21 |
| Capital market openness | 0.46 | * | 0.16 | 0.53 | 0.15 | 0.11 |
| Settlement and transaction costs | -0.06 | | 0.26 | 0.35 | 0.41 | 0.08 |

*Note:* Significance of coefficients at 1% (\*\*\*), 5% (\*\*), and 10% level (\*) based on a two-tailed T-test.

were not significant enough to move countries' overall Wilshire total labor scores between 2002 and 2003.

I find strong evidence that countries with low scores in 2002, particularly countries excluded from CalPERS investment portfolio, worked hard to raise their scores over the year. The simple correlation coefficient between the 2002 score and the change in the score—between 2003 and 2002) was -0.48, demonstrating the agency of nation states to determine their fate. The question is whether such nation state agency is a product of development measured by GDP change over a specific time period? In order to address this question, I regressed the difference in countries' scores between 2003 and 2002 on their total scores in 2002 as well as the real GDP growth rate in 2002, and obtained the following equation (coefficient of determination equals 0.57, *t*-values are reported in parentheses).

$$\text{Score } 2003{-}2002 = 0.46 \ (2.6) - 0.216 \ (-2.45) \ \times \ \text{Score } 2002 + 0.017 \ (1.9)$$
$$\times \ \text{GDP growth rate}$$

Therefore, although I find a significant positive relationship between the change in a country's score and its economic growth, there is an even more significant negative relationship between the starting level of the score and the change in the score. In other words, while economic development provides increased opportunity for countries to improve their standards, GDP growth in and of itself is not the principal driver of the change in these emerging market countries' total scores. To a large extent, irrespective of their economic fortunes as indicated by the GDP change, countries that started with low scores in 2002 and subsequent exclusion from CalPERS' emerging markets portfolio, demonstrated a greater responsiveness to converge to global standards than countries with high scores. From these data I draw the conclusion that nation states are key agents in the process of convergence to global standards and are more influenced by potential ability to attract future investment than by endowments of the past.

## Conclusion

Using access to CalPERS and the unique data set of emerging market countries from Wilshire, there is evidence to back investor intuition that applying both financial and extra-financial standards to entire countries within emerging markets portfolios acts as a catalyst to raise standards beyond those currently consistent with these countries' regulatory frameworks.[11] I show that countries' convergence to uniform global standards is accelerated by external investors' threat of capital flight. I call this ability to leverage external investment the global institutional investment value chain, and I map both its development and its potential to raise global standards of behavior.

The results have significant implications for conceptualizing the dynamic nature of the global standard-setting process. Along the institutional investor value chain I find nation states remain key actors in global standard setting. Absent global government, most global corporate standards continue to be voluntary with material disclosure remaining patchwork at best. In contrast, national regulatory regimes provide legitimate and legally binding standards on all corporate entities operating within their defined national boundaries. While these standards may well be minimum requirements, raising them directly improves both global standards of behavior and by extension global equity and social justice outcomes. I find that countries and their regulatory regimes are central to external capital investment decisions and that by using their investment leverage, pension funds can have a profound impact on the global standard-setting process.

CalPERS' real-world investment decision to screen twenty-seven emerging market countries based on both country and market factors draws important conclusions as to the impact of the global institutional investor value chain on global standards of behavior. I use this real-world model to interrogate assumptions about the drivers of external finance decisions. Furthermore, I test for the validity of the global institutional investment value chain and its ability to leverage investment decisions to raise global standards.

Based on this data set, I dispute the presumptions made by La Porta and his colleagues (1997) that legal regimes are settled, and their origins are key determinants for external investment decisions in emerging markets. I find that within emerging markets, countries' legal origins play a limited role in shaping external finance decisions and initial country ratings are more likely determined by the country's relative wealth as measured by per capita purchasing power parity (PPP) GDP. The speed by which countries regulate convergence to global standards is the mechanism that attracts and holds today's global investors and countries' ability and willingness to adopt these standards in the face of capital market exclusion is unrelated to the origins of their legal regimes.

Moreover, consistent with the institutional investor value chain hypothesis, this chapter shows that when excluded from foreign investment emerging market countries raise their corporate practices and standards to attract that investment in the future. To this extent countries are active agents that shape their own futures. Even in the single time period examined, countries with the lowest scores in 2002 and therefore excluded from CalPERS' investment, dramatically improved their scores in 2003. Nation states demonstrated their agency capabilities in the face of real capital flight.

Finally, I tested the leverage capability of institutional investors to determine if convergence to global standards was primarily influenced by improved economic growth within the emerging market country rather then by external demands. I found that while initial low per capita PPP GDP may well be a drag on countries' ability to change and while economic development does provide increased opportunity for countries to improve their standards, GDP growth in and of itself is not the principle driver of the change in these emerging market countries' total scores. Improvement in scores by emerging market countries was a direct result of exclusion from foreign investment.

These conclusions help us define the global institutional investment value chain and its ability to leverage investment in order to promote convergence to global standards. Along the value chain these active institutional agents are shaping the world.

# 6

# The Way Forward

There is little doubt that corporate engagement has become germane both for pension funds and for the larger financial community. Hardly a day goes by without some mention in the financial press of initiatives undertaken by pension fund boards and administrators designed to influence the standards of firms they hold in their investment portfolios. This book offers insight into why pension funds undertake such action and what results are achieved both for the pension funds themselves and more broadly for the corporations with which they engage.

Pension fund corporate engagement represents a rise of institutional investors' influence generally, and pension fund investors' specifically. It could be argued that such pension fund influence is simply the result of their massive exponential asset growth within the capital market. But size alone is not enough to back this claim. If pension funds failed to use their impact on capital markets any differently than in the period before their rapid growth, one could not claim to be witnessing a new process. But evidence suggests these funds are indeed behaving in a new way in capital markets.

Pension funds are able to behave as unitary economic agents within the financial system and are using their influence to raise corporate standards. To act as single economic agents requires the pooling of enormous assets under the direction of a unified board of trustees allowing for decisions to be backed up by the full weight of the asset base of the fund. In 2007, public sector defined benefit pension plans are in the lead on using corporate engagement to raise corporate standards. With the decline in growth of defined benefit pension plans, their influence may wane in the future, but currently their absolute size makes them effective in influencing firm-level decisions. Large private sector and defined contribution plans are increasingly taking up corporate engagement as a successful investment strategy (see, for example, the $440 billion TIAA-CREF as of September 2007). The expansion of corporate engagement in these other types of funds is important considering that in 1997, defined contribution plans surpassed defined benefit plans in asset size in the United States. Defined contribution plans and mutual funds are the fastest growing among U.S. institutional investors. Small policy changes are already having an impact with these investors and the requirement to vote and disclose proxy voting by mutual funds has led to increased support for shareholder resolutions on executive compensation. Such policy changes that bring about much needed transparency with mutual funds and defined contribution pension plans may well stimulate active ownership on their part in the future.

In light of governance failures that began in 2000 absentee owners were seen as contributing to the problem with direct calls on institutional investors, particularly pension funds, to become more engaged with companies they hold in their investment portfolios. As a result, pension funds have been at the forefront of the calls for CEO resignations (e.g., the resignation of the New York Stock Exchange chair Richard Grasso or American Airlines CEO Donald Carty); the tightening of corporate rules (e.g., at the SEC) in the post Sarbanes-Oxley period; the reduction in executive compensation packages (e.g., at GlaxoSmithKline); and demands for better board governance standards (note the role of pension funds, particularly public sector plans in removing the chair of Disney Board of Directors Michael Eisner). One might also argue that the corporate governance scandals that began in 2001 contributed to pension funds' growing influence while simultaneously undermining government as the sole providers of oversight in the market.

The effectiveness of pension fund corporate engagement is further enhanced by pension funds' newfound willingness to work in coalition. Although each fund holds only a fraction of outstanding equity in any one firm, together they make up sufficient size to make their influence felt. Such coalitions are able to move beyond simply monitoring management decision making into the realm of directly influencing management decision-making outcomes.

### Long-Term Investors

Although pension fund corporate engagement's shifting power dynamic within the firm would make for an interesting study in and of itself, it would not be a dramatic change if decisions made by institutional investors were identical to those made by firm-level managers. Beginning in the period following the collapse of the TMT bubble in 2000, many pension fund officials are increasingly concerned with the long-term rather than short-term share value of the stocks they hold in their equity portfolios. This shift is primarily due to pension funds' increasing exposure to losses incurred from short-term behavior in the market, and the realization that equity markets will not produce such heady returns in the future.

Until the late 1990s, pension fund managers held a short-term view of the financial market (see particularly Romano 2001 and Shiller 2002 on this point). They traded frequently (a practice known as churning), contributing to ever-escalating rates of market turnover. Such trades were driven by a single-minded focus on the quarterly performance of stocks in their portfolio. Pension fund money managers often saw their own compensation and bonuses linked to quarterly performance of stocks under their management, and portfolio mandates were often terminated by pension funds when target rates of return were not met. Several studies in the 1990s found that the quarterly performance demands of pension fund money managers directly contributed to corporate managers' short-term decisions at the expense of long-term performance.

Although pension fund money managers were not exempt from their role in driving the market to short-term extremes in the 1990s, soaring levels of executive compensation linked to short-term value of stock options were more instrumental in driving corporate decision making during this time. Throughout the 1990s, stock market values moved upward at a dizzying pace, all based on short-term, quarterly reports with little care about long-run fundamental value. As long as portfolios had 25 percent annual returns neither pension fund officials, nor corporate managers were overly concerned with short-termism in the market.

The collapse of the TMT bubble in 2000, followed by the failure of several corporate giants, both in the United States and Europe, demonstrated that a single-minded focus on short-term value has real consequences in the long run. The growing stock market dominance of Anglo-American pension funds meant that when short-term decisions met long-term outcomes, pension funds suffered enormous losses in their portfolios. Many pension funds lost up to a quarter of their assets between 2000 and 2002.

It would be fair to say that without experiencing direct losses in their investment portfolios, the majority of pension fund officials would be unlikely to shift their investment time horizon from that of corporate managers. But the events that followed the 2000 stock market collapse have indicated to most pension funds that the long-term nature of their liabilities, sometimes stretching over fifty years, requires them to have equity investment time horizons much longer than those of most corporate managers. Unfortunately for pensioners and plan beneficiaries, it has taken the direct impact of short-term losses for many pension fund officials to reorient themselves toward longer-term corporate objectives. In light of these dramatic losses we are beginning to see a shift toward longer-term objectives, with pension funds increasingly measuring success based on rolling three- and five-year averages of equity performance. That said, most pension funds remain conflicted by the need to shift their investment time horizon to the long-term while simultaneously measuring portfolio performance against short-term and sometimes even quarterly performance benchmarks. Consider the flood of pension fund monies into hedge funds over the past four years. The need for short-term results has been further acerbated by low returns from equities combined with underfunding ratios for many pension funds. In addition, many public sector funds are under legislated mandates to achieve a certain level of annual return. This has required a "search for alpha" that clouds the expressed intent of the pension fund to become a "long term investor."

Still, many pension funds are using corporate governance levers to reorient corporate decisions toward longer-term objectives. For example, many pension funds now demand that stock options granted to corporate senior executives (for many the real driver of short-term market behavior) either be judged against industrywide benchmark performance, have longer-term payout horizons, or be stopped altogether.

This new sensitivity to long-term share value is reflected in the two pension funds profiled in this book. Both California Public Employees Retirement System's (CalPERS) and Universities Superannuation Scheme's (USS) mission statements declare a concern for the long-term share value of their portfolios. Such sentiment (now common in many Anglo-American pension plans) is backed by considerable action on the part of these two funds. The use of corporate engagement is indicative of greater awareness of the need to match assets against long-term liabilities. CalPERS pays considerable attention to corporate governance issues in the companies in which they invest. They are motivated by the link between good corporate governance and better financial returns over time (Anson et al. 2003; Nesbitt 1995). CalPERS is so closely associated with corporate governance monitoring that such returns have been dubbed the "CalPERS effect." One could argue that such forays into corporate governance paved the way for increased sensitivity to the long-term fundamentals of the firm (also known as value investing) and are reflected in CalPERS' other campaigns to raise the standards of the firms and even countries in which they invests.

As discussed in chapter 4, the UK-based USS is also committed to the long-term investment strategies and uses corporate engagement to challenge firms in their investment portfolio. USS' first major corporate engagement campaign was focused on global climate change. Considering the long-term nature of such an issue this focus provides ample evidence of their long time horizon. USS also uses its market position to interest other financial market players in adopting a long-term approach to investment. In 2003, they established a widely reported global competition ("Managing Pension Fund Assets as if the Long-Term Really Did Matter") among money managers in order to demonstrate how to build greater consideration for the long-term objectives into portfolio management. USS asked money managers to develop portfolio ideas for a fictitious €30 billion mandate based on the long-term investment. USS received eighty-eight entries from numerous money managers and interested individuals. One of the most influential organizations that developed out of this competition is the Enhanced Analytic Initiative in which pension funds commit a percentage of their analysts' mandates to those who use extra-financial as well as financial criteria in investment selection.

Both of these pension funds have played an active role in new global coalitions working toward greater sustainable investing practices including increased transparency and long-termism. The coalitions include the Carbon Disclosure Project, the Principles of Responsible Investing, and the Enhanced Analytics Initiative.

## Raising Corporate Standards

In the wake of the 2000 stock bubble collapse and the failure of several corporate giants, pension funds, policy makers, and even the public became sensitized to the need to raise standards of corporate behavior. The failures at Enron, WorldCom, Ahold, and Parmalat highlighted the need for corporate governance standards and have been the most obvious arena in which pension fund investors use corporate engagement to raise firm-level standards. But rather than altruism, in most cases raising these standards is a direct result of the correlation between positive corporate governance and long-term share value. Most pension fund managers interviewed felt that such corporate engagement was, "making capitalism more efficient" or "reducing the principal-agent problem."

In contrast, pension fund engagement designed to raise social and environmental aspects of firm behavior is less frequently observed. Although such action could be described as socially responsible investing, most pension funds eschew this label and prefer to think of these social and environmental demands as providing insurance against future risk and uncertainty. Most pension funds show concern about corporate standards after they experience direct losses in the market. Just as pension funds' corporate governance concerns followed the collapse of Enron, CalPERS' interest in social and environmental standards in their emerging markets portfolio was motivated by portfolio losses in the period following the 1998 collapse of the Asian markets.

## Policy Implications

One need look no further than the 2004 OECD Principles of Corporate Governance to see the enormous impact pension fund corporate engagement has on policy. In 1995, when the OECD first drafted its corporate governance guidelines, there was a single reference to institutional investors in the document. By 2004, the redraft of these guidelines included three pages on the influence of institutional investors in maintaining confidence in financial markets.

The 2000 collapse of the TMT stock bubble emphasized the fact that financial markets work best when owners actively monitor the corporations in which they invest. Given that transaction costs inherent in monitoring are prohibitive to small investors, most of this responsibility is falling to institutional investors, with large, usually public sector, defined benefit pension funds leading the charge. Such corporate engagement carries with it significant policy implications for pension funds (and other institutional investors) for corporations and for market regulators.

Pension funds are increasingly aware of the need to engage firms in their portfolio, but because individual funds hold only a small amount of outstanding equity in each firm, pension funds must be prepared to work in coalition with each other to be truly effective. This requires them to take a less competitive stance vis-à-vis their peers. It also means pension funds that use corporate engagement to raise standards and by extension share value, must accept "free riders" who benefit from these initiatives without bearing any of the costs. The direct costs involved in corporate engagement should not be underrated, particularly as most pension funds pride themselves on keeping their administrative costs as low as possible. Both policy stances are new for pension funds that in the past were characterized as "lone wolves" unable or unwilling to cooperate with others (see, for example, Coffee 1997; and O'Barr and Conley 1992 for detailed description of pension funds' inability to cooperate with one another).

Furthermore, while active ownership and engagement have been encouraged by market regulators, to become truly effective in market oversight, private sector pension funds and other large institutional investors, particularly mutual funds, must join with public sector pension funds in corporate engagement. To date these investors have not been active in this arena. It is presumed that private sector pension funds do not want to engage other corporations for fear of their own company or industry coming under similar scrutiny. Mutual funds and large external money managers, who solicit significant business from the private sector, are seen to be reluctant to openly criticize corporations for fear of losing current or future portfolio mandates. Given the decline in defined benefit pension plans over time, other types of institutional investors, particularly those that manage defined contribution pensions and mutual fund managers, will need to become active owners if corporate engagement is to remain a strong force going forward.

The policy implications of pension fund engagement for corporations are equally significant. Essentially such engagement uses external leverage to raise firm-level standards of behavior. Such demands result in stronger corporate governance within the firm and higher standards of corporate responsibility, both of which have been linked to long-term share value. What is encouraging about pension fund corporate engagement is that it lengthens the time horizon for firm-level decision making, which is crucially important for a well-functioning capitalist economy. Faced with these demands, firms must become more responsive to owners and less prone to the knee-jerk reaction that management knows best.

Although we can expect to see increased regulatory pressure on firms as a result of corporate engagement, responsive corporations will also act voluntarily to raise their environmental, social, and corporate governance standards in anticipation of increased external scrutiny. We are already seeing a voluntary corporate response to the corporate governance failures over the last few years. Voluntary reporting of stock options as expenses, the separation of board chair from CEO are just two examples of corporations' increasing responsiveness to external scrutiny.

We should also expect to see corporations providing increased transparency of both financial and extra-financial (i.e., social and environmental) aspects of firm behavior. Pension fund corporate engagement requires that more information on firm-level decision making be available in order to facilitate efficient investments. Forward-thinking companies will provide this information in anticipation of changes in regulatory and investment practice.

The advent of pension fund corporate engagement also has policy implications for financial markets and regulators. Markets do not work well without oversight and monitoring of corporate managers by owners (Bogle 2005). Such intuition stands in contrast to the 1990s when regulators assumed that well-structured reporting rules could provide the required oversight of corporate managers. In seeking additional monitoring from owners, regulators understand that given institutional investors' dominance in financial markets and ability to overcome the transaction costs, these investors should be encouraged. This requires financial regulators to ensure that minority shareholder rights are both in place and enforced.

In some cases regulators are expanding shareholder rights. Institutional investors are also being encouraged and in some cases coerced into using already available tools of corporate engagement. Here I point specifically to new SEC regulations to make disclosure of proxy voting by mutual funds mandatory, a move encouraged by many large public sector pension funds in the United States. Such activity has the effect of both mandating engagement (in the past many mutual fund investors failed to vote their proxies or voted only with management) and in making financial markets more transparent.

We expect to see mandatory increased transparency not just for institutional investors but across financial markets. In order to satisfy the information needs of pension funds and other institutional investors, mandatory reporting of both financial and extra-financial aspects of firm behavior will be necessary. Greater material disclosure informs all the actors along the institutional investment value chain. One expected result is increased corporate performance ratings and benchmarking that includes a fuller range of financial and extra-financial risk factors. It could be argued that Moody's and Standard and Poor's inclusion of corporate governance ratings is a step in this direction.

One of the interesting findings of this investigation of pension fund corporate engagement is the continued importance of countries and their regulatory regimes, as providers of minimum standards corporations must meet to satisfy investor demands. Despite the predictions that global finance would come to dominate, global investors still require nation state actors to impose rules and raise standards in the companies in which they invest.

Two final caveats must be raised as to potential negative impacts pension fund corporate engagement could have within the financial market. First, I have been careful to note that pension fund investors should limit their influence on firm-level decisions to raising the standards of the firm in which they invest. It would be a mistake for these investors to begin to engage in day-to-day business decisions that rightfully belong to management. Pension fund officials do not have the expertise or detailed knowledge of investee firms to take on this function. Such an attempt would result in inefficient use of resources and would in the end be harmful to plan beneficiaries who must remain the central concern for pension fund managers.

Second, pension funds themselves must become aware of their own standards of governance, transparency, and accountability as their influence in the market grows. Pension fund governance lags the demands they make on corporations and to be credible they must ensure their own governance can withstand scrutiny. This will require more transparency in decision making and greater accountability of pension fund managers to their own beneficiaries.

That said, pension fund corporate engagement offers a unique opportunity to raise the environmental, social, and governance standards of corporate behavior. By bringing increased oversight to firm-level managers, combined with recognition of long-term risks investors face, there is a potential for a dramatic shift in corporate behavior. Pension fund corporate engagement is key to such a shift in the future.

# Table A. I
# CalPERS Focus List demands 2000–2007

| Company | Demands | Trans-parency | Account-ability |
|---|---|---|---|
| **2007 Focus List** | | | |
| Corinthian Colleges, Inc (COCO)** | Lack of board accountability—the company would not seek shareowner approval to remove the company's classified board structure | | yes |
| International Paper Corporation (IP) | Characteristics of an entrenched board | | yes |
| | Unresponsive to shareowners | | yes |
| | Would not agree to remove the staggered "classified" board structure, eventhough a proposal at the 2006 AGM received 79% of "for" votes | | yes |
| | Would not agree to remove supermajority voting requirements that pertain to articles of incorporation | | yes |
| | | | yes |
| | Would not agree to seek shareowner approval for any future poison pill | | yes |
| Marsh & McLennan Companies, Inc. (MMC) | Would not adopt a policy to require shareowner approval for any future poison pill | | yes |
| | Would not agree to seek shareowner approval when the present value of an officer's severance exceeds 2.99 times base + bonus | | yes |
| | CalPERS seeks shareowner ratification of any severance agreement that provides severance benefits with a total present value exceeding 2.99 times the sum of the officer's base salary plus target bonus | | yes |
| Tenet Healthcare Corporation (THC) | Ranked in the bottom 10% of companies in Economic Value Added "EVA" performance base CalPERS' 2007 Focus List Screen | | |
| | Would not agree to remove supermajority voting ments that pertain to articles of incorporation. | | yes |
| Dollar Tree Stores (DLTR) | Lack of board accountability—the company would not seek shareowner approval to remove the company's classified board structure | | yes |
| | Would not agree to seek shareowner approval to remove the supermajority voting requirements that pertain to the articles of incorporation and bylaws | | yes |

| Company | Demands | Trans-parency | Account-ability |
|---|---|---|---|
| Dollar Tree Stores (DLTR) (cont.) | Limited shareowner rights—would not agree to grant shareowners the right to call special meetings or act by written consent | | yes |
| | Would not agree to implement "double triggers" on equity payouts so that during a change in control, unvested equity would convert to the new company (without termination) | | yes |
| | CalPERS seeks to remove the company's supermajority voting requirements that pertain to the articles and bylaws | | yes |
| Kellwood Corporation (KWD)** | Lack of board accountability—the company would not seek shareowner approval to remove the company's classified board structure | | yes |
| | Concern over shareowner rights—would not agree to seek shareowner approval to remove the supermajority voting requirements that pertain to the articles of incorporation and bylaws | | yes |
| | CalPERS seeks to remove the company's classified or "staggered" board structure CalPERS believes that annual elections for directors provide greater accountability to shareowners | | yes |
| Sanmina-SCI Corporation (SANM) | Sanmina-SCI ranked in the bottom 10% of companies in Economic Value Added "EVA" performance based upon CalPERS' 2007 Focus List Screen | | |
| | Would not agree to expedite expiration of poison pill and adopt approval policy on future pill, or seek shareowner approval for existing poison pill | | yes |
| | Would not agree to adopt a clawback policy to recapture bonus and incentive payments in the event of officer fraud or misconduct | | yes |
| Tribune Company (TRB) | Concerns over high level of anti-takeover defenses—the company would not agree to seek shareowner approval to remove the classi-fied board structure; remove supermajority voting requirements that pertain to the articles of incorporation and bylaws; adopt a policy that requires shareowner approval for its existing or future poison pill | | yes |
| | Would not agree to implement majority voting for directors | | yes |
| | Would not agree to adopt a clawback policy to recapture bonus an incentive payments in the event of officer fraud or misconduct | | yes |
| | Would not agree to seek shareowner approval when the present value of an officer's severance exceeds 2.99 times base+bonus | | yes |
| | CalPERS seeks to remove the company's super-majority voting requirements that pertain to the articles and bylaws | | yes |

| Company | Demands | Trans-parency | Account-ability |
|---------|---------|---------------|-----------------|
| EMC Corporation (EMC) | Would not agree to seek shareowner approval when the present value of an officer's severance exceeds 2.99 times base+bonus | | yes |
| | Would not agree to grant shareowners the right to call special meetings or act by written consent | | yes |
| Eli Lilly & Company (LLY) | Shareowners may not amend the bylaws. The company would not agree to amend this egregious provision | | yes |
| | Would not agree to grant shareowners the right to call special meetings or act by written consent | | yes |
| | Would not agree to seek shareowner approval for existing or future poison pills | | yes |
| | CalPERS seeks to allow a simple majority of shareowners (51%) the right to amend the bylaws | | yes |
| Sara Lee Corporation (SLE) | Shareowners may not amend the bylaws. The company would not agree to amend this egregious provision | | yes |
| | Would not agree to seek shareowner approval to remove the supermajority voting requirements that pertain to business combinations, director removal, and shareowners' ability to act by written consent | | yes |

## 2006 Focus List

| Company | Demands | Trans-parency | Account-ability |
|---------|---------|---------------|-----------------|
| Brocade Communication System (BRCD) | Stock has declined by over 68% in the last 5 years ending March 31st | | |
| | Shareowner rights are limited and the company employs excessive takeover defenses | | |
| | Shareowners may not call special meetings or act by written consent; the company has a classified board structure, 67% supermajority voting requirements for shareowners to amend key portions of the charter bylaws, and a poison pill that is not shareowner approved | | yes |
| | No majority voting for directors | | yes |
| | Concern over lack of audit/fiancial expertise and strategic industry expertise on the board | | |
| | Three directors recently stepped down, which leaves only 2 members on the audit committee | | yes |
| | CalPERS seeks to remove the 67% super-majority requirements necessary to amend key portions of the company's charter and bylaws | | |
| | CalPERS believes that a majority of shareowner votes should be required to amend the charter and bylaws | | yes |

| Company | Demands | Trans-parency | Account-ability |
|---|---|---|---|
| Mellon Financial (MEL) | Excessive takeover defenses: classified board structure, 75% supermajority requirements to amend key portions of the bylaws, and a poison pill that is not shareowner approved | | |
| | No majority voting for directors | | yes |
| | Total severance benefits in the event of a change in control will exceed 2.99 times the sum of the officer's base salary plus target bonus | | yes |
| | Mellon would not permit an independent director to meet with CalPERS staff | | yes |
| Cardinal Health Inc. (CAH) | Excessive takeover defenses: supemajority requirements of 75% are in place to amend the company's bylaws. Cardinal Health does not have a policy to require shareowner approval for any future poison pill | | yes |
| | No majority voting for directors | | yes |
| | Total severance benefits in the event of a change in control will exceed 2.99 times the sum of the officer's base salary plus target bonus | | yes |
| | The auditor is not ratified by shareowners | | yes |
| | CalPERS seeks shareowner ratification of any severance agreement that provides severance benefits with a total present value exceeding 2.99 times the sum of the officer's base salary plus target bonus | | yes |
| OfficeMax Inc. (OMX) | Excessive takeover defenses: supermajority voting requirements of 80% are in place to amend the bylaws, and the poison pill is not shareowner approved | | yes |
| | Concern over inadequate retail and financial related expertise on the board | | yes |
| | No majority voting for directors | | yes |
| | OfficeMax would not permit and independent director to meet with CalPERS staff | | yes |
| | CalPERS seeks to remove the 75% super-majority requirements necessary to amend key portions of the company's bylaws. CalPERS believes that a majority of shareowner votes should be required to amend the company's bylaws. | | yes |
| Clear Channel Communication Inc. (CCU) | Concern over board culture: The Compensation Committee Chairman and the Nominating/Governance Committee Chairman have served for over 22 years | | yes |
| | Concern over inadequate international business and technology related expertise on the board | | yes |
| | No majority voting for directors | | yes |
| | No "double triggers" on equity severance in the event of a change in control. A double trigger would provide that an executive must be terminated following a change in control before the vesting of equity will accelerate | | yes |

| Company | Demands | Trans-parency | Account-ability |
|---|---|---|---|
| Sovereign Bancorp Inc. (SOV) | Excessive takeover defenses: the company has a classified board structure, 80% supermajority requirements to amend certain provisions of the charter and bylaws, and a poison pill that is not shareowner approved. Sovereign's poison pill has a very low triggering ownership threshold of 9.9% | | yes |
| | Concern over board culture: The lead director has served for over 19 years. Severance agreements are in palce for non-employee directors, a practice that is highly uncommon | | yes |
| | CalPERS seeks to remove the company's classified or "staggered" board structure | | |
| | CalPERS believes that annual elections for directors provides greater accountability to shareowners | | yes |

## 2005 Focus List

| Company | Demands | Trans-parency | Account-ability |
|---|---|---|---|
| American International Group | Increased financial risk due to a declining stock price, accounting misstatements | | |
| | An excessive number of employee and affiliated directors with Board seats | | yes |
| | Shareowners need more transparency about the Board's executive succession planning | yes | |
| | Seeks to amend bylaws at its May 2005 annual meeting to require an independent chairperson and at least two-thirds of the Board be independent directors | | yes |
| AT&T | AT&T's stock has lost more than 74% of value in the last 5 years ended March 31 | | |
| | Seeks to require at its 2005 annual meeting shareowner approval of any severance payout that exceeds 2.99 times the sum of the executive's base salary and bonus | | yes |
| Delphi | Delphi's stock has significantly underperformed its peer group for the last 1, 3, and 5 year period ended March 31 | | |
| | Company announced that it overstated cash flow from operations by $200 million in 2000 and overstated pre-tax income in 2001 by $61 million | | |
| | SEC and FBI investigating the company | | |
| | Lack of correlation between executive pay and financial performance, and lack of executive or director holding requirements | | |
| | Seeks to amend Delphi's bylaws at its May 2005 annual meeting to ban any current or former director from being re-elected if the director opposed declassifying the Board following last year's annual meeting | | |
| Novell | Novell's stock has lost 47% of value for the one-year period ended March 31, during a time when their industry peers gained on average 6.2% | | |

| Company | Demands | Trans-parency | Account-ability |
|---|---|---|---|
| Novell (cont.) | Seeks to amend Novell's bylaws to require that at least 50% of senior executive equity compensation be performance-based and that performance metrics be fully disclosed to shareowners. This proposal was supported by 31% of the shareowners at Novell's April 14 annual meeting | | yes |
| Weyerhaeuser Company | Poor response to multiple majority approved shareowner proposals but not implemented by the Board. Shareowner proposals to declassify the Board were approved by a majority of shareowners in 2000, 2002 and 2003 | | |
| | In 2004, the company ran a management proposal to declassify the Board but recommended that shareowners vote "Against" the proposal. Company remains unresponsive to CalPERS requests to eliminate its supermajority voting requirement which requires 67% of shareowners to amend its restated article of incorporation, as well as the ability to amend the classified board structure | | |
| | Seeks to declassify the Weyerhaeuser Board at the April 21 annual meeting and to require annual election of directors | | yes |

## 2004 Focus List

| Company | Demands | Trans-parency | Account-ability |
|---|---|---|---|
| Emerson Electric Company | Formalize director evaluations | | yes |
| | Commit to independent board members and reduce the employee representation on the Board | | yes |
| | Provide an analysis of retaining former CEO Charles Knight as Chairman and Board member and commit to renegotiating the excessive terms of Mr. Knights contract and perquisites | | yes |
| | Seek shareholder approval of the company's poison pill | | yes |
| | Seek shareholder approval to eliminate the supermajority requirements and declassify the Board by the 2005 annual meeting | | yes |
| | Tie a significant portion of the Company's long-term compensation to performance-based measures | | yes |
| | Improve communication and transparency of good governance initiatives | yes | |
| Maytag Corporation | Adopt formal equity ownership requirements for directors | | yes |
| | Eliminate the supermajority voting requirements contained in the Eleventh Article of the Certificate of Incorporation and work with CalPERS and a proxy solicitor to help ensure that the required vote is obtained | | yes |

| Company | Demands | Trans-parency | Account-ability |
|---|---|---|---|
| Maytag Corporation (cont.) | Seek shareholder approval of the Company's poison pill | | yes |
| | Declassify the Board by the 2005 annual meeting | | yes |
| Royal Dutch Shell | Transport to undertake a rigorous and wide-ranging re-examination of the Group and how it is managed. Develop a charter with objectives, committee members, tasks and feedback timetables | | |
| | This Board level Committee should address the (1) role of a Group CEO, (2) management succession, (3) nomination of independent directors and succession process of the Board, and (4) composition of the Group's boards | | yes |
| | Establish a policy that allows shareholders open access and nominations to the Board | | yes |
| | Remove reserves from compensation "Scorecards" | | |
| | Reinforce the necessity for compliant reserves bookings | | yes |
| | Group Disclosure Committee should be enhanced with Group Legal Director and quarterly access to the Committee of Managing Directors | | yes |
| | Develop and foster a culture of compliance, ethics and appropriate conduct | | yes |
| The Walt Disney Company | Instill greater Board independence | | yes |
| | Develop a Board approved succession plan for CEO, Board Chair, and top officers | | yes |
| | Tie a significant portion of the Company's long-term compensation to performance-based measures | | yes |

## 2003 Focus List

| Company | Demands | Trans-parency | Account-ability |
|---|---|---|---|
| Gemstar-TV Guide International | Conduct a formal governance review using an independent external consultant | yes | |
| | Make a formal commitment to maintain a majority of independent directors | | yes |
| | Adopt CalPERS definition of an independent director | | yes |
| | Commit to 100% independent directors on key committees | | yes |
| | Adopt a formal board/self-evaluation process | yes | yes |
| | Add at least one new independent director | | yes |
| | Executive compensation policy | yes | |
| JDS Uniphase Corp | Conduct a formal governance review using an independent external consultant | yes | |
| | Make a formal commitment to maintain a majority of independent directors | | yes |
| | Conduct Board needs assessment and add members with appropriate skill sets | yes | |
| | Adopt CalPERS definition of an independent director | | yes |

| Company | Demands | Trans-parency | Account-ability |
|---|---|---|---|
| JDS Uniphase Corp (cont.) | Develop and seek shareholder approval for a formal executive compensation policy | yes | |
| | Seek shareholder approval to declassify Board | | |
| | Seek shareholder approval to maintain the Company's poison pill | | |
| | Maintain separate roles of Chairman and CEO | | yes |
| Manugistics Group, Inc. | Conduct a formal governance review using an independent external consultant | yes | |
| | Make a formal commitment to maintain a majority of independent directors | | yes |
| | Adopt CalPERS definition of an independent director | | yes |
| | Maintain 100% independent directors on key committees | | yes |
| | Hold executive session where independent directors meet alone at each board meeting | yes | |
| | Separate Chairman and CEO | | yes |
| | Adopt a formal board/self-evaluation process. | yes | |
| | Maintain 100% independent directors on key committees | | yes |
| | Hold executive session where independent directors meet alone at each board meeting | yes | |
| | Separate Chairman and CEO | | yes |
| | Adopt a formal board/self-evaluation process | yes | |
| | Review director compensation considering mix of cash and equity based components | | |
| | Seek shareholder approval for executive compensation policy | yes | |
| Midway Games, Inc. | Add two new independent directors | | yes |
| | Conduct a formal governance review using an independent external consultant | yes | |
| | Make a formal commitment to maintain a majority of independent directors | | yes |
| | Adopt CalPERS definition of an independent director | | yes |
| | Make a formal commitment to maintain 100% independent directors on key committees | | yes |
| | Develop and seek shareholder approval for a formal executive compensation policy | yes | |
| | Adopt board/self-evaluation process | yes | |
| | Separate the roles of Chairman and CEO | | yes |
| | Adopt formal equity ownership guidelines | | |
| Xerox Corporation | Add three new independent directors | | yes |
| | Consider eliminating Executive Committee | | yes |
| | Adopt CalPERS definition of an independent director | | yes |
| | Maintain 100% independent directors on key committees | | yes |
| | Split Chairman and CEO | | yes |
| | Adopt board evaluation process | yes | |
| | Develop and seek shareholder approval for executive compensation policy | | yes |

| Company | Demands | Trans-parency | Account-ability |
|---------|---------|:-------------:|:---------------:|

## 2002 Focus List

| Company | Demands | Trans-parency | Account-ability |
|---------|---------|:-------------:|:---------------:|
| Cincinnati Financial | Perform a formal governance review | yes | |
| | Review and revise the current Director compensation plan | yes | |
| | Adopt a resolution requiring the Board consist of a majority of independent directors | | yes |
| | Key committees be composed exclusively of independent directors | | yes |
| | Appoint a lead independent director | | yes |
| Gateway | Conduct a formal governance review using an external consultant | yes | |
| | Request that the Board de-classify itself into one class of directors | | |
| | Key committees be comprised exclusively of independent directors | | yes |
| | Separate the Chairman and Chief Executive Officer positions | | yes |
| Lucent Technologies | Expand the Board by several members | | yes |
| | Request that the Board de-classify itself into one class of directors | | |
| | Review all anti-take-over provisions used by the company | | |
| | Consider adopting CalPERS' definition of independence | | yes |
| | Adopt a resolution requiring the Board consist of a majority of independent directors | | yes |
| | Clearly define Henry Schacht's role on the Board | | yes |
| NTL, Inc. | Perform formal governance review using an external consultant | yes | |
| | Establish a formal Nominating Committee | | yes |
| | Adopt a resolution requiring the key committees be exclusively independent directors | | yes |
| | Adopt a resolution requiring that the Board consist of a majority of independent directors | | yes |
| | Review the current Director compensation plan | yes | |
| Qwest | Perform formal governance review using an external consultant | yes | |
| | Request that the Board de-classify itself into one class of directors | | |
| | Adopt a resolution requiring the key committees be exclusively independent directors | | yes |
| | Request that only one Chairman sit on the Board | | yes |

## 2001 Focus List

| Company | Demands | Trans-parency | Account-ability |
|---------|---------|:-------------:|:---------------:|
| Circuit City | Commit to maintain a majority of independent directors | | yes |
| | 100% independent directors on key committees | | yes |
| | Phase out the former CEOs of the Board as their current term expires | | yes |

| Company | Demands | Trans-parency | Account-ability |
|---|---|---|---|
| Circuit City (cont.) | Change the description of lead director to include independent | | |
| | Conduct a Board self-evaluation using an external consultant | yes | |
| Lance | Appoint a lead independent director | | yes |
| | 100% independent directors on key committees | | yes |
| | Conduct a Board self-evaluation using an external consultant | yes | |
| Metromedia | Commit to maintain a majority of independent directors on the Board | | yes |
| | 100% independent directors on key committees | | yes |
| | Conduct a Board self-evaluation using an external consultant | yes | |
| | Eliminate the management fee relationship | | yes |
| Ralcorp | Commit to maintain a majority of independent directors on the Board | | yes |
| | 100% independent directors on key committees | | yes |
| | Conduct a Board self-evaluation using an external consultant | yes | |
| Warnaco | Commit to maintain a majority of independent directors on the Board | | yes |
| | 100% independent directors on key committees | | yes |

## 2000 Focus List

| Company | Demands | Trans-parency | Account-ability |
|---|---|---|---|
| Advanced Micro Devices | Board's Chairperson be an Independent Director | | yes |
| Bob Evans Farms | Committed to separate the Chair and CEO positions | | yes |
| | Elected a lead independent director | | yes |
| Crown Cork and Seal | Adopted a bylaw to require that a majority of directors be independent | | yes |
| A.G. Edwards | Will restructure the board to include a majority of independent directors | | yes |
| | Will establish a Nominating Committee consisting of independent directors and the CEO | | yes |
| | Will make director compensation more competitive | | yes |
| | Will eliminate any involvement of management in establishing the compensation of the CEO | | yes |
| First Union Corporation | Will designate a lead independent director | | yes |
| | Agreed that future Nominating Committee will not include CEO | | yes |
| Intergraph Corporation | Will appoint three additional independent directors | | yes |
| | Will appoint a lead independent director | | yes |
| | Will form a key committees comprised solely of independent directors | | yes |
| J.C. Penney | Declassify the Board | | |

| Company | Demands | Trans-parency | Account-ability |
|---------|---------|---------------|-----------------|
| Lone Star Steak House | Majority of the Board be comprised of Inde-pendent Directors | | yes |
| | Will perform annual evaluations of the CEO | yes | |
| | Will study the current compensation of the Board and portion paid in stock | | |
| | Will form a Nominating Committee comprised of solely independent directors | | yes |
| Phycor | Will maintain a majority of independent directors | | yes |

# Table A.2
# CalPERS shareholder resolutions 1987–2000

| | | | | Anti-takeover device | Board independence |
|---|---|---|---|---|---|
| 1987–88 | Consolidated Freightways | Anti-Poison Pill Proposal | Received 42% of vote | yes | |
| | Gillette | Anti-Greenmail Proposal | Passed | yes | |
| | Great Northern Nekoosa | Anti-Poison Pill Proposal | Received 28% of vote | yes | |
| | Ryder System | Confidential Voting | Received 22% of vote | yes | |
| | Texaco Repeal | Anti-Takeover Provisions | Passed | yes | |
| | US Air Group | Anti-Poison Pill Proposal | Received 48% of vote | yes | |
| 1988–89 | Avon Products | Anti-Poison Pill Proposal | Received 40% of vote | yes | |
| | Consolidated Freightways | Anti-Poison Pill Proposal | Received 42% of vote | yes | |
| | Continental Corp. | Confidential Voting | Passed | yes | |
| | First Interstate Bancorp | Confidential Voting | Passed | yes | |
| | Great Northern Nekoosa | Anti-Poison Pill Proposal | Passed | yes | |
| | Halliburton | Anti-Poison Pill Proposal | Received 35% of vote | yes | |
| | Lockheed | Opt out of Delaware's Anti-Takeover | Received 23% of vote | yes | |
| | Ryder System | Confidential Voting | Received 42% of vote | yes | |
| | Texaco | Shareholder Advisory Committee | Passed | | Yes |
| | US Air Group | Anti-Poison Pill Proposal | Received 48% of vote | yes | |
| | Wells Fargo | Reincorporate in California | Withdrawn | yes | |
| | Whirlpool | Confidential Voting | Received 37% of vote | yes | |
| 1989–90 | Avon Products | Create Shareholder Advisory | Received 45% of vote | | Yes |
| | Consolidated Freightways | Anti-Poison Pill Proposal | Received 45% of vote | yes | |
| | EG&G | Confidential Voting | Passed | yes | |
| | Halliburton | Anti-Poison Pill Proposal | Received 47% of vote | yes | |
| | Ryder System | Confidential Voting | Passed | yes | |
| | US Air Group | Anti-Poison Pill Proposal | Received 40% of vote | yes | |
| | Whirlpool | Confidential Voting | Received 45% of vote | yes | |
| 1990–91 | Avon Products | Create Shareholder Advisory | Passed | | Yes |
| | General Motors | Majority Independent Directors | Passed | | Yes |
| | Hercules | Confidential Voting | Passed | yes | |
| | Inland Steel | Confidential Voting | Passed | yes | |
| | ITT | Executive Compensation | Passed | | Yes |

| | | | | Anti-takeover device | Board independence |
|---|---|---|---|---|---|
| 1990–91 (cont.) | Scott Paper | Reincorporate out of Pennsylvania | Passed | yes | |
| | Sears | Shareholder Advisory Committee | Passed | | Yes |
| | WR Grace | Executive Compensation | Passed | | Yes |
| | Whirlpool | Confidential Voting | Received 42% vote | yes | |
| 1991–92 | American Express | Executive Compensation | Passed | | Yes |
| | Dial Corp. | Executive Compensation | Passed | | Yes |
| | Hercules | Performance/New | Passed | | Yes |
| 1992–93 | Advanced Micro Devices | Independent Chair | Withdrawn | | Yes |
| | Chrysler | Independent | Withdrawn | | Yes |
| | First Mississippi | De-Stagger Board | Withdrawn | yes | |
| | Pennzoil | SAC | Proposal excluded by SEC | | |
| 1993–94 | Boise Cascade | De-Stagger Board | Withdrawn | yes | |
| | US Shoe Corp. | De-Stagger Board | Passed | yes | |
| | USX Marathon Group | Lead Director | Withdrawn | | Yes |
| | Zenith | Lead Director | Withdrawn | | Yes |
| 1994–95 | Boise Cascade | De-Stagger Board (Precatory) | Received 44% of vote | yes | |
| | Melville | Independent Chair (Precatory) | Withdrawn | | Yes |
| | Navistar International | Indep. Chair (Precatory)/ De-Stagger | Withdrawn/Withdrawn | yes | Yes |
| | Oryx Energy | De-Stagger Board (Precatory) | Passed | yes | |
| | Zurn Industries | De-Stagger Board | Withdrawn | yes | |
| 1995–96 | Archer Daniels Midland | Majority Indep. Directors | Received 40% of vote | | Yes |
| | Oryx Energy | De-Stagger Board | Withdrawn | yes | |
| | Stride Rite Corp. | De-Stagger Board | Withdrawn | yes | |
| | US Surgical Corp. | Independent Chair | Withdrawn | | Yes |
| 1996–97 | Bassett Furniture Ind. | Independent Chair | Withdrawn | | Yes |
| | Fleming | De-Stagger Board | Withdrawn | yes | |
| | Reebok | De-Stagger Board | Passed | yes | |
| | Rollins Environmental | Independent Directors | Withdrawn | | Yes |
| 1997–98 | Advanced Micro Devices | Independent Chair | Received 28% of vote | | Yes |
| | International Flavors & Fragrances | Independent Chair | Withdrawn | | Yes |
| | Electronic Data Systems | Independent Chair | Received 21% of vote | | Yes |
| | MAXXAM | De-Stagger Board | Received 15% of vote | yes | |
| | Sybase Inc. | De-Stagger Board | Received 67% of vote | yes | |
| | Stewart Stevenson Se | De-Stagger Board | Withdrawn | yes | |
| | Michaels | Independent Directors | Withdrawn | | Yes |
| 1998–99 | Mandalay Resort Group | Majority Independent Directors | Received 26.4% of vote | | Yes |
| | Cummins Engine | Independent Audit Committee | Withdrawn | | Yes |
| | Pacific Century Financial | Majority Independent Directors | Withdrawn | | Yes |
| | Pioneer Natural Resource | De-Stagger Board | Withdrawn | yes | |
| | Sierra Health | De-Stagger Board | Withdrawn | yes | |
| | St. Jude Medical, Inc. | Majority Independent Directors | Passed | | Yes |

| | | | Anti-takeover device | Board independence |
|---|---|---|---|---|
| | Tyson Foods, Inc. | Eliminate Dual Classes of Stock | Received 5% of the vote    yes | |
| 1999–2000 | Advanced Micro Devices | Independent Chair | Received 25.5% of the vote | Yes |
| | Crown Cork & Seal Co | Majority Independent Directors | Withdrawn | Yes |
| | A.G. Edwards, Inc. | Majority Independent Directors | Withdrawn | Yes |
| | First Union Corporation | Independent Chair | Withdrawn | Yes |
| | Intergraph Corporation | Majority Independent Directors | Withdrawn | Yes |
| | Lone Star Steakhouse | Majority Independent Directors | Passed (64.5% of the vote) | Yes |
| | J.C. Penney Company | De-Stagger Board | Received 69.5% of the vote    yes | |
| | Phycor, Inc. | Majority Independent Directors | Withdrawn | Yes |

# Abbreviations and Acronyms

| | |
|---|---|
| BP | British Petroleum |
| CalPERS | California Public Employees Retirement System |
| CalSTRS | California State Teachers' Retirement System |
| CDP | Carbon Disclosure Project |
| CEO | Chief Executive Officer |
| CERES | Coalition for Environmentally Responsible Economies |
| CII | Council of Institutional Investors |
| CSR | Corporate Social Responsibility |
| DB | Defined Benefit |
| DC | Defined Contribution |
| EAI | Enhanced Analytics Initiative |
| EITI | Extractive Industries Transparency Initiative |
| ERISA | Employee Retirement Income Security Act |
| ESG | Environmental, Social, and Governance |
| EVA | Economic Value Added |
| FDI | Foreign Direct Investment |
| GAAP | Generally Accepted Accounting Principles |
| GE | General Electric |
| GDP | Gross Domestic Product |
| GSK | GlaxoSmithKline |
| GRI | Global Reporting Initiative |
| IASB | International Accounting Standards Board |
| ICCR | Interfaith Center for Corporate Responsibility |
| ILO | International Labor Organization |
| ISO | International Organization for Standardization |
| ISS | Institutional Shareholder Services |

| | |
|---|---|
| KLD | Kinder, Lydenberg and Domini |
| NGO | Non-Governmental Organization |
| OECD | Organization for Economic Cooperation and Development |
| P/E | Price/Earnings Ratio |
| PRI | Principles for Responsible Investment |
| RI | Responsible Investing |
| SAM | Sustainable Asset Management |
| SEC | Securities and Exchange Commission |
| SRI | Socially Responsible Investing |
| TMT | Technology, Media and Telecommunication |
| UNEP | United Nations Environment Programme |
| USS | Universities Superannuation Scheme |
| WTO | World Trade Organization |

# Glossary of Terms

Given the multidisciplinary nature of this research, I provide a brief glossary of frequently used terms in the context in which they are used.

ACCOUNTABILITY. Used in corporate governance to establish the reporting requirements from firm managers to firm owners. Usually such accountability mechanisms include the role of boards of directors in monitoring management decision making. Accountability mechanisms reflect the allocation of power within the firm.

ACTIVE INVESTMENT STYLE. Active investment money managers believe they are able to use available information to select stock that is undervalued by the market. They hope that such stock selection will result in outperformance of the market (see Alpha) over time. Active investment costs more to administer than passive investments, which mimic the market as a whole. As a result in periods of high stock market returns active investment managers rarely outperform the market, particularly in Anglo-American stock markets. However, during market downturns their track record is much better.

ALPHA. This is a measure of excess return of a stock portfolio adjusted for risk as measured against the total market return. The presence of alpha is the result of weak market efficiency, where everything about the firm is not fully known and factored into the price. Such information asymmetry leads to mispricing in the market.

ANGLO-AMERICAN (ALTERNATIVELY ANGLO-SAXON). Used to define the financial system of the United States, United Kingdom, and other Commonwealth countries. Past common law origins, use of English, and strong public financial markets, as well as the presence of pools of capital generated from pension savings are all hallmarks of the Anglo-American financial system.

BENCHMARK. A standard portfolio against which other portfolios can be measured. In order to judge a money manager's or a portfolio's performance one must be able to make a standard comparison. Benchmarks are widely used in the pension fund industry to judge a money manager's performance. Investment mandates are terminated if money managers consistently underperform predetermined benchmarks. While overperformance might be a measure of too much volatility in the portfolio, money managers are seldom fired for exceeding these targets.

BENEFICIARIES. Members of a pension plan who hold a claim for pension benefits upon retirement.

BETA. A statistical measurement of the volatility or sensitivity of rates of return on a portfolio or in comparison to a market index. A beta of 1, for example, means that the security and the market both return the same rate.

BRAND IMAGE (ALTERNATIVELY CORPORATE IMAGE OR IDENTITY). Name, symbol, or word created by the manufacturer of a product to identify its product in the marketplace. Brand images often associate products with a set of desirable values and characteristics, and single out the product from the competition.

CAPITAL MARKETS (ALTERNATIVELY FINANCIAL MARKETS). Where securities, either debt or equity, are bought and sold.

CONSUMER MARKETS (ALTERNATIVELY PRODUCT MARKETS). Where goods and services are purchased.

CORPORATE ENGAGEMENT. The use of one's ownership position to influence firm-level decision making.

CORPORATE GOVERNANCE. The system of rules and structures that oversees the running of a corporation. Alternatively, the system of rules by which owners are assured the return of their investment or the allocation of power among managers, owners, and boards of directors.

CORPORATE SOCIAL RESPONSIBILITY (ALTERNATIVELY CORPORATE RESPONSIBILITY). Recognizes the claims of all stakeholders on corporate behavior. Generally associated with raised standards of corporate behavior.

DEFINED BENEFIT (DB) PENSION PLANS. A type of pension plan where upon retirement the beneficiaries receive a pension based on a formula of length of service and percentage of best annual salary level achieved. The assets are pooled and invested on behalf of all plan members.

DEFINED CONTRIBUTION (DC) PENSION PLANS. A type of pension plan where upon retirement the beneficiaries receive a pension based on the total amount contributed to the individual's account by both employee and employer plus its earnings.

EMERGING MARKETS. The financial markets of newly developing economies.

EQUITY PREMIUM. Theoretically, the increased return from an equity security over a debt security, which represents the return to capital of increased risk inherent in equity investing. There is increasing debate as to the strength of the equity premium over the last twenty years see Diamond (1999) on this point.

FIDUCIARY DUTY. A relationship of trust and a standard of care defined by law that an individual who manages money for another person's benefit must fulfill.

FINANCIAL PERFORMANCE (ALTERNATIVELY SHARE VALUE). The performance of a company measured in terms of the risk-adjusted rate of return captured in its share price. The share price is said to reflect the present value of the future stream of revenue generated by the company.

FOREIGN DIRECT INVESTMENT. The acquisition abroad of physical assets such as plant and equipment, with operating control residing in the parent corporation.

GROWTH INVESTMENT STYLE. Looks for companies and sectors of the economy expected to have above-average prospects of growth in earnings and profitability. Such stock often sells with above average price/earnings ratios as opposed to value style investments (see below). The dot-com bubble was fueled by expectations of future growth in the high tech sector, with price earnings ratios at unheard of levels. In some cases these companies never made a profit, yet traded at multiples of one hundred times projected earnings.

INDEX FUNDS. Investment products that mimic the returns of large public stock market indexes such as the S&P 500 or the FTSE100. These funds became increasingly popular in the 1990s when large market indexes were generating returns of 20 percent and more. Given such returns, money managers were seldom able to outperform the index through active management in the 1990s.

INSTITUTIONAL INVESTORS. Organizations that invest on behalf of others to whom they have a fiduciary duty. The major institutional investors covered in this study are pension funds; others include mutual funds, insurance companies as well as banks, investment companies, and endowments. Institutional investors have come to dominate global financial markets.

LONG TERM. In accounting this term is used to indicate a time period greater than one year. Most financial analysts would not use the term for anything longer than ten years, beyond which one cannot predict outcomes.

PASSIVE INVESTMENT STYLE. Passive investment money managers choose investment instruments that mimic the stock market as a whole. Generally these funds are constructed to follow the returns of a major public index such as the S&P 500. These money managers believe that you cannot outperform the stock market through stock selection, in other words they do not believe in alpha.

POISON PILL. An anti-takeover device that gives the current shareholders of a firm the right to buy shares of the firm or shares of anyone who acquires the firm at a deep *discount* of their fair *market value.* Such rights make the takeover of the firm unattractive to new owners. This action is named after the cyanide pill that secret agents are instructed to swallow if capture is imminent.

PORTFOLIO SCREENING. Is often associated with socially responsible investing (see below). Here a set of selection criteria beyond financial requirements is externally imposed on the portfolio. One can find both positive and negative screening—positive screening looks for certain types of firms to be included in the portfolio, while negative screening excludes certain types of investments. Most common negative screens exclude tobacco, alcohol, and armaments, though Islamic screened funds also exclude banks.

RATING AGENCIES. Organizations that supply investors with knowledgeable information about the security for sale. Rating agencies provide impartial information on either debt or equity instruments. In the past most ratings were determined only on the basis of financial information provided by the firm. More recently rating agencies include a variety of corporate governance factors in their assessment of firm performance. Both Standard and Poor's and Moody's now include this data. Several smaller rating agencies have recently begun to specialize in social and environmental aspects of firm performance. Rating agencies are vitally important for informing investment decision making.

REPUTATION. Used to denote the capital market's reaction over time to a series of announcements (or surprises) regarding the corporation. In capital market terms such announcements generally indicate whether reported earnings in a given time period matched the expected earnings for the firm. Over time, failure to meet expected earnings results in a loss of share value and a diminished reputation in the market.

SHORT TERM. Used in accounting the term defines a period of less than one year. Much has been written about the increased pressure through the 1980s and 1990s on corporations to focus on short-term rather than long-term financial performance. Fueled by extravagant executive compensation through stock options and investors' demands for positive quarterly earnings, decisions that favored short-term immediate returns were often chosen over other longer-term projects resulting in an erosion of share value over time. The collapse of the TMT bubble (see below) began to reorient managers and investors away from the short-term and toward long-term value.

SOCIALLY RESPONSIBLE INVESTING (SRI). Considers aspects of firm behavior beyond simply their financial returns. Most socially responsible investors look for firms that display strong social, ethical, and environmental standards of behavior. While some SRI investors eschew corporations whose products run counter to their personal ethics such as armaments, nuclear, tobacco, gambling, or alcohol, others seek companies that display best-of-sector standards. This latter approach is strengthened by the links between strong environmental and social standards of firm behavior and positive rates of return. In the United States, total SRI is estimated at $2 trillion, or one in every eight dollars of investments.

STAKEHOLDERS. A corporation's stakeholders are a cross section of society affected by a firm's behavior and to whom the firm is responsible. Generally stakeholders are said to include shareholders, employees, customers, communities, and the environment. Recognizing the rights of stakeholders underpins a much broader conception of the firm's role in society than simply generating excess profit for the benefit of shareholders.

TECHNOLOGY, MEDIA, AND TELECOMMUNICATIONS (TMT) BUBBLE. Defines the run up in the United States and United Kingdom stock market through the 1990s directly attributable to the escalating stock price for TMT companies. As with stock bubbles over the last three centuries (i.e., the South Sea Bubble and the 1920s) such bubbles are marked by "irrational exuberance" as to the real value of the company. For a detailed description of irrational exuberance see Shiller (2000)). The stock price becomes disengaged from its underlying fundamentals and its price soars, driven by ever-increasing demand. Just as with previous stock bubbles, the TMT stock bubble was not able to sustain itself and stock markets fell dramatically between 2000 and 2002.

TRANSACTION COSTS. Denotes time, effort, and financial costs involved in monitoring the behavior of firm-level managers. For widely dispersed owners who own only a fraction of any one company's stock the costs of monitoring the activities of the firm would far exceed the value of their holdings, making such an effort inefficient. Only when the costs involved in monitoring are less than the payoff will such monitoring take place.

TRANSPARENCY. A key component of corporate governance that deals with making information about the firm publicly available. Corporate disclosure usually takes the form of annual filings of information required by law. Such disclosure includes key financial reporting and other items that have material bearing on the performance of the firm going forward. Increasingly, particularly following the corporate governance scandals of Enron and Worldcom, shareholders and other stakeholders are requiring companies to make their actions more transparent.

VALUE INVESTMENT STYLE. Looks for firms believed to be undervalued in the market or trading at lower price/earnings ratios than their true value. This style of investor seeks out such firms in order to gain alpha (see above). This strategy is predicated on the understanding that over time such firms will gain value because the underlying fundamentals of the firm are strong. Increasingly such fundamentals include both financial and extra-financial aspects of the firm.

# Notes

## Chapter 1. Understanding Pension Fund Corporate Engagement

1. Studies that back this belief include ABI 2001: Bauer et al. 2002, 2005; EPA 2000, Gluck and Becker 2005; Griffin and Mahon 1997; Guerard 1997; Kiernan and Levinson 1998; Monks 2001; Pava and Krausz 1995; Porter 1995; and UNEP 2001. Evidence of high standards of governance and its correlation with out-performance has been discussed by Anson et al. 2003; Bebchuk et al. 2004; Gompers et al. 2003; Junkin and Toth 2006; Nesbitt 1994, 1995; and Smith, 1996.

2. Institutional investors include pension funds, investment and mutual funds, insurance companies, and banks.

3. Corporate engagement is the term used to describe the use of legally defined corporate ownership rights by shareholders to raise the firms' standards. It puts pension funds at the center of a contested terrain between today's corporate managers and owners. While corporate engagement represents a power shift from managers to owners, power does not shift without a struggle and backlash to corporate engagement.

4. All figures drawn from Conference Board (2007).

5. It must be noted that although pension funds have grown significantly over the past twenty-five years and remain the largest type of institutional investor in the United States at 39 percent of total assets (as of 2005), their growth rates are dwarfed when we compare them to mutual funds, which have increases in size from 2.6 percent of total institutional investor assets in 1980 to 25 percent in 2005 (Conference Board 2007). For a detailed examination of the impact of mutual funds on financial markets in the United States see John C. Bogle (2005).

6. TIAA-CREF has long been a corporate governance champion, building on the 2006 survey of its membership it has begun to actively promote its socially responsible investment and community investing portfolio with its members (TIAA-CREF 2007). TIAA-CREF serves as a model for other DC plans.

7. CalPERS deliberately uses the term shareowner rather than shareholder to highlight their position as long-term owners of publicly traded corporations. "CalPERS is not simply a passive holder of stock. We are a "shareowner," and take seriously the responsibility that comes with company ownership" (CalPERS 2007b).

8. Short-term investment strategies gaining increased popularity in the "search for alpha" include hedge funds investment and stock lending, for example. Many activist hedge funds are notoriously short term, pressing companies to shift strategies and drop business lines to achieve quick changes in share value. Yet in 2006 U.S. pension funds held $50 billion in hedge funds up from just $5 billion in 2001 (Pensions and Investments 2007).

9. A recent competition by Universities Superannuation Scheme, one of the largest pension funds in the United Kingdom, challenged money managers to create a portfolio that reflected a long-term view of wealth creation. The entries from over forty conventional money managers around the globe make for fascinating reading (2003).

10. Of the twenty-five largest pension plans in the United States, nineteen are public sector DB pension plans.

11. However, in 2007 the Illinois legislator's Sudan divestment policy was found to be too restrictive in scope and was overturned in court. That same year, Illinois has subsequently moved to require divestment in Iran.

12. In November 1999 the World Trade Organization (WTO) met in Seattle. The meeting was targeted by thousands of anti-globalization protestors who wanted to draw attention to the destructive effects of globalization on developing countries around the world. Protestors took to the streets in angry and violent confrontation with WTO officials and police. This protest was one of many between 1999 and 2001.

13. Verizon CEO had made $109 million between 2002 and 2007 despite a total return to shareholders of -5 percent.

14. The EAI was developed after the USS held a fictional mandate competition "Managing as if the Long Term Really Mattered." Signatories to the EAI realized that financial analysts would see a cash commitment from the institutional investor as incentive to use extra-financial data in their work. In this case capital equals commitment on the part of pension fund investors.

15. In the United States, even with a majority of votes, a minority shareholder resolution only requires management to take such action under advisement. In the United Kingdom and other common law countries management must act on a minority shareholder resolution that receives the majority of shareholder votes. Dual class voting structures and large management shareholdings make achieving an outright majority of votes difficult.

## Chapter 2. Intersecting Interests

1. Studies indicate that divesting of stock, particularly small positions, does not change the price of capital for the firm. In most cases sellers who divest for ethical reasons are matched by buyers who are willing to accept current prices for what are often dubbed "sin" stocks (e.g., tobacco).

2. The Carbon Disclosure Project, UNEP PRI, climate change campaigns, Wal-Mart shareholder campaigns, and Sudan divestment campaigns are all examples of recent synergies between traditional SRI advocates and pension fund investors.

3. These companies included Altria Group, Google, Hewlett-Packard, and Microsoft (Conference Board 2007).

4. See, for example, the ruling in *Board of Trustees of the Retirement System v. Mayor of Baltimore.*

5. *The Board of Trustees of the Retirement System v. Mayor of Baltimore* case states, "Indeed, courts have long recognized that property embodies social relationships, as well as economic ones" ("Divestment Upheld," 817).

6. Ralph Nader helped mount a campaign against General Motors following his 1965 report *Unsafe at Any Speed.* GM placed Ralph Nader under surveillance at the time and subsequently Nader sued and won a settlement against GM for their actions. In 1970 Nader and his coalition began a minority shareholder campaign to propose three new members for GM's board. Though unsuccessful it became a model for consumer-led activism in the United States.

7. In 1998 the U.S. Department of Labor issued an opinion letter on Socially Responsible Investing by pension funds governed under ERISA. The "Calvert Letter" details pension funds ability to undertake investments with "collateral benefits."

8. The legislation for Sudan divestment has been modeled on California, which restricted divestment in companies engaged directly in Sudanese conflict. It is important to note that too broad a legislative restriction can result in successful law suits against the pension fund as was the case with MassPRIM's Burma divestment in 2000.

## Chapter 3. The Economic Inefficiency of Secrecy

1. Sharing previously secret information allows subsequent decisions on the part of all actors to become more efficient. In essence transparency lowers the agency costs inherent in the separation of ownership from control (Williamson 1985).

2. Corporate governance has many definitions. It is said to be the means by which a company is controlled (LaPorta et al. 1999); the method by which suppliers of capital ensure returns on investment (Shleifer 1997); or the means of decision making and power allocation among shareholders, senior managers, and boards of directors (Roe 2000). All three definitions describe the allocation of power within the corporate structure.

3. *Dodge v. Ford Motor Co.,* Michigan Supreme Court, 1919, 204 Mich. 459, 170 NW 668.

4. In 2003 the SEC began considering new rules that would allow shareholders access to the proxy through which to nominate directors, much to the objection of corporate America. But as of July 2007 backlash to the role of activist owners has resulted in the SEC stalling on this proposal.

5. One of the damning conclusions of the U.S. Senate Investigation Committee into the collapse of Enron was the fact that "The independence of the Enron Board of Directors was compromised by financial ties between the company and certain Board members" (U.S. Senate 2002, 54).

6. The unexpected losses at hedge fund Amaranth in September 2006 were estimated at $6 billion after a risky bet was (wrongly) made on energy prices.

7. In 2003 the OECD convened the Global Forum on International Investment: Encouraging Modern Governance and Transparency for Investment. This body is increasingly focused on transparency and has highlighted this in both its

Guidelines for Multi-National Enterprises and in the OECD Principles of Corporate Governance. With Europe's Parmalat scandal following on the heels of the U.S. Enron and Worldcom debacles, the guardians of good corporate governance are increasingly aware of the importance of transparency within these structures.

8. As discussed in chapter 1, "Wall Street Walk" is the term given to selling a security when unhappy with its financial return.

9. One of the most successful proxy voting coalitions to date has been the overturning of the senior executive compensation package at the global pharmaceutical corporation GlaxoSmithKline in 2003. It drew together pension funds from the United Kingdom, the United States, and Canada in a coordinated and highly public display of pension fund power. The resignation of NYSE chair Richard Grasso is another case of pension funds influence in coalition.

10. In 1996 Michael Smith first used the term "CalPERS effect" to describe the wealth creation impacts on firms included in the annual CalPERS' focus list of underperforming, poorly governed firms. It can be argued that such impacts were the result of short-term rather than long-term decisions taken by the firms in the Focus List. It can also be argued that these underperforming firms had nowhere to go but up. However, Smith highlighted the linkage between placement on CalPERS' focus list and subsequent wealth impacts for shareholders.

11. Economic Value Added (EVA) is a company's after-tax net operating profit, minus its cost of capital for one year. By using EVA and stock performance, CalPERS pinpoints companies where poor market performance is due to underlying economic performance problems as opposed to industry or extraneous factors.

12. CalPERS' shareholder view of the corporation was strong enough to warrant protests from Parisian workers when Bill Crist paid a routine visit to France in 2000 (Tagliabue 2000).

13. CalPERS' Senior Investment Officer Christianna Wood included all aspects of CalPERS' corporate governance campaign in a recent speech titled, "Transparency Requirements for Institutional Investors."

14. One senior executive at CalPERS noted that, "fixing the agency problem is 98 percent of the value of corporate governance campaigns." But wrongly concluded that therefore "Corporate governance is not political."

15. I find this trend in the United States with the largest public sector pension funds such as CalPERS, CalSTRS, NYCERS, New York State, Wisconsin, Connecticut; in the United Kingdom with the second largest fund BT Pension Fund through their wholly owned money managers Hermes; and in Canada's CPPIB, Caisse de Depot, and Ontario Teachers Pension Plan.

16. A TIAA-CREF survey of its beneficiaries demonstrates the high level of plan members' interest in SRI strategies for their investments (as long as financial performance is not sacrificed).

17. CalPERS' total portfolio in relational investing is $2.6 billion and has an annualized return of 14.2 percent (net annualized since inception in 1996). Its benchmark global equity index has returned 9.3 percent net annualized over the same period for an out-performance of 4.9 percent (CalPERS 2004).

18. Corporate governance advocates, academics, and government regulators are just three of the groups calling on pension funds to provide greater monitoring and oversight. Regulators such as the SEC (Kinder 2004) and the OECD (2004) are calling on pension funds and other institutional investors to play this role.

19. A 2007 study of AFSME, the Corporate Library, and Shareholder Education Group found that in 2006 twenty-nine mutual fund companies supported 45 percent of shareholder resolutions on executive compensation. In 2005 they supported only 27 percent of these resolutions. This is important as mutual funds currently account for more than 25 percent of outstanding equity in the United States. In combination with activist pension funds, this makes a substantial voting block.

## Chapter 4. Why Do They Care?

1. Hollinger International was a media holding company that owned the *Chicago Sun-Times*, among its twenty newspapers. Following a campaign initiated by institutional investor Tweedy-Brown, the SEC charged CEO Conrad Black and associates with allegedly "looting" $400 million from the newspaper. Black was convicted on several charges in July 2007. Two weeks later, Black's Canadian holding company, Hollinger Inc., filed for bankruptcy.

2. In my research on pension fund corporate engagement, this is one of just a few instances where plan members were the catalyst for such intervention. In the vast majority of cases, plan members have little power. Exit, voice, and loyalty are not options for plan members; their participation is taken for granted by plan administrators (Clark 2004).

3. There is no evidence that screening-out makes any difference to firms' access to or price of capital. Stocks sold through such a strategy are bought by other investors without regard to seller's intentions. Portfolio investors rarely hold more than thirty basis points of any individual stock; only in a few instances is ownership so concentrated in the hands of a few investors that a concerted selling strategy adversely affects stock prices.

4. Most pension funds that use their ownership position to raise firm-level standards first identify corporate governance (reputation) concerns with which to engage companies. Once active in the process of engagement, their focus extends to broader social and environmental (earnings-related) aspects of firm behavior.

5. Considering this chapter's overarching argument and focus on corporate engagement, I do not consider the nature and scope of proxy votes in advancing social and environmental issues. Even so, there is increasing evidence to the effect that high-profile shareholder resolutions can have significant impacts on corporate managers' behavior over a wide variety of issues. For useful overviews of the theory and practice of proxy voting, see Maug (1999) and Romano (2001). On the institutional basis of proxy voting, see http://www.corpgov.net/ and http://www.issproxy.com/.

6. Building on helpful suggestions made by Teresa Ghilarducci and Ewald Engelen, such an approach could be described as one of voice rather than exit (Hirschman 1970). Here the pension fund seeks to gain insurance against reputational damage. In contrast, CalPERS could be said to use exit or "strike" to

pursue its objectives. Such exit is costly and crude. It is understood that rather than insurance, CalPERS perceives the value of the stock to be already discounted for the negative behavior and uses such methods to raise share value.

7. Two of the three external money managers CalPERS' uses in its emerging market screening have significantly outperformed their benchmarks since inception. Such outperformance speaks to both the value of active fund management and the value of reputation in these markets.

8. Witness the adverse impact on Foreign Direct Investment to the Philippines when CalPERS announced in 2002 that it would divest itself from that emerging market (Chan-Lau et al. 2004).

## Chapter 5. Global Standards and Emerging Markets

1. Emerging markets are defined by the World Bank (2003) as countries with a 2001 gross national income per capita below $9,206.

2. U.S. financial accounting standards were developed in direct response to the 1929 U.S. stock market collapse. Preliminary accounting standards were initially developed by the newly formed Securities and Exchange Commission in the early 1930s. These standards were strengthened in 1938 with the development of the Committee on Accounting Procedure, the Accounting Principles Board in 1959 and Financial Accounting Standards Board in 1973. The standards and opinions set by these three bodies over sixty-five years are recognized as the U.S. GAAP, one of the global measurements of traditional financial accounting.

3. The legislation implementing the Swedish-, Swiss-, German-, and French-funded capital pools within their social security system all include provision for social, ethical, and environmental impacts to be considered in investment decision making.

4. The Global Sullivan Principles are still in use today as a set of standards for anti-discrimination in the workplace. Initially developed by Reverend Sullivan during the South Africa anti-apartheid campaign, investors were instrumental in calling for these principles as part of their conditions of investment.

5. The 1999 UK legislation (implemented in 2000) required transparency and disclosure in investment practice; it did not require pension funds to use social, ethical, or environmental criteria. However, it did force UK pension funds to take a position on these criteria even if that position was negative. The net result was that 70 percent of UK pension funds developed a positive statement on using these criteria, though most indicated that financial concerns superseded these extra-financial measurers.

6. CalPERS emerging market universe is defined as countries that fall below 2001 gross national income per capita of $9,206 (CalPERS 2003), with investable capital markets defined as having American Depository Receipts or Global Depository Receipts traded in approved markets. The twenty-seven countries chosen are based on an amalgamation of the 2001 emerging markets indices of three major international market index publishers: MSCI, Standard and Poor's, and Financial Times.

7. Wilshire and Associates is the primary consultant used by CalPERS to rate its emerging market portfolio. It uses a total score that rates countries on a 1-to-3

scale across seven major market and country factors, with being 3 the highest score.

8. Because of the low number of observations, the Russian legal origin family, China, and Hungary were excluded from this part of the analysis. Poland was assigned to the German legal origin family.

9. We used GDP per capita in 2002 based on PPP (CIA World Factbook 2003).

10. I use the term path dependence to reference the effects of initial endowments, past commitments, or acquired knowledge on subsequent actions and decisions.

11. It could be argued that countries with the lowest Wilshire score had nowhere to go but up, while high scoring countries had no room for improvement. However, our data shows that some high scoring countries also continued to improve their score. Therefore, the results are not skewed for the under-performing countries.

# References

Association of British Insurers (ABI) (2001). "Investing in Social Responsibility." Report. London: ABI.

Anson M., T. White, and H. Ho (2003). "The Shareholder Wealth Effects of CalPERS Focus List." *Journal of Applied Corporate Finance* 15 (3): 8–17.

Arthur, W. B (1992). *Increasing Returns and Path Dependence in the Economy.* Ann Arbor: University of Michigan Press.

Associated Press (2002, January 29). Available at www.recordsearchlight.com/newsarchive/20020129topstate024.shtml. Accessed May 2nd 2003.

Bakan, J. (2004). *The Corporation: The Pathological Pursuit of Profit and Power.* New York: Free Press.

Bauer, Robert, Nadja Gunster, and Roger Otten (2003). "Empirical Evidence on Corporate Governance in Europe." ABP Investments and Maastricht University Working Paper, Brussels.

Bauer, Robert, Kees Koedijk, and Roger Otten (2002). "International Evidence on Ethical Mutual Fund Performance and Investment Style." ABP Investments and Maastricht University Working Paper, Brussels.

—— (2005). "The Eco-Efficiency Premium Puzzle in US Equity Markets." *Financial Analysts Journal* 61 (2): 51–63.

Bebchuk, Lucian A., Alma Cohen, and Allen Ferrell (2004). "What Matters in Corporate Governance." John M. Olin Center for Law, Economics, and Business of Harvard University Working Paper, Cambridge, MA.

Becker, Eric, and Patrick McVeigh (2001). "Social Funds in the United States: Their History, Financial Performance, and Social Impacts." In *Working Capital: The Power of Labor's Pensions,* ed. A. Fung, T. Hebb, and J. Rogers. Ithaca: Cornell University Press.

Berle, Adolf A., and Gardiner C. Means (1933). *The Modern Corporation and Private Property.* New York: Macmillan.

Blackburn, Robin. (2003). "Grey Capital and the Challenge of Pension Finance." Paper presented at the conference Pension Fund Capitalism and the Crisis of Old-Age Security in the United States. Center for Economic Policy Analysis, New School University.

Bogle, John C. (2005). *The Battle for the Soul of Capitalism*. New Haven, CT: Yale University Press.

Brancato, Carolyn (1994, September). "Brancato Report on Institutional Investment," 3rd ed., vol. 1. Conference Board, New York.

Brandeis, L. D. (1914). *Other Peoples' Money—and How the Bankers Use It*. New York: F. A. Stokes.

Bushee, Brian (1998). "Institutional Investors, Long Term Investment, and Earnings Management." Harvard Business School Working Paper 98–069, Cambridge, MA.

Carbon Disclosure Project (2007)"Carbon Disclosure Project Report 2006." Available at http://www.cdproject.net/cdp5reports.asp. Accessed July 2007.

California Public Employees Retirement System (CalPERS) (2000). Charles P. Valdes's Speech on Principles of Corporate Governance. Sacramento.

—— (2003). Investment Committee Agenda item 6-b. Report, February 18. Sacramento.

—— (2004). Investment Committee, Report. Available at http://www.calpers.ca.gov/index.jsp?bc=/utilities/search/search.xml. Accessed April 10 2005.

—— (2005). "CalPERS Seeks Greater Disclosure of Environmental Data Under New Corporate Governance Initiative." Press Release, February 14.

—— (2006). CalPERS and CalSTRS Report on Oil and Gas Sector Response to Carbon Disclosure Project.

—— (2007a). Policy on Permissible Equity for Emerging Equity Markets. May 14.

—— (2007b). CalPERS Shareowners Forum. Report. Available at http://www.calpers-governance.org/forumhome.asp. Accessed June 15, 2007.

Chan-Lau, Jorge A., Donald J. Mathieson, and James Y. Yao (2004). "Extreme Contagion in Equity Markets," IMF Staff Papers, International Monetary Fund, 51 (2): 386–408.

Clark, Gordon L. (2000). *Pension Fund Capitalism*. Oxford: Oxford University Press.

—— (2003). *European Pensions and Global Finance*. Oxford: Oxford University Press.

—— (2004). "Pension Fund Governance: Expertise and Organizational Form." *Journal of Pension Economics and Finance* 3(2): 233–53.

Clark, Gordon L., and Tessa Hebb (2004). "Corporate Engagement: The Fifth Stage of Capitalism." *Relations Industrielles/Industrial Relations* 59: 142–69.

Coffee, John C. (1991). "Liquidity Versus Control, the Institutional Investor as Corporate Monitor. *Columbia Law Review* 91: 1277–368.

—— (1997). "The Folklore of Investor Capitalism." *Michigan Law Review* 95: 1970–89.

—— (2002). "Racing Toward the Top?: The Impact of Cross-Listings and Stock Market Competition on International Corporate Governance." Columbia Law and Economics Working Paper 205. Columbia University, New York.

CIA World Factbook (2003). Available at http://www.cia.gov/cia/publications/factbook/. Accessed November 5, 2003.

Conference Board (2007). "The 2007 Institutional Investment Report." New York.

Crist, William (2003). Private interview, January 16. Sacramento, CA.

Davis, E. Philip, and Benn Steil (2001). *Institutional Investors.* Cambridge, MA: MIT Press.

Deakin, S. (2005). "The Coming Transformation of Shareholder Value." *International Review of Corporate Governance* 13 (1): 11–18.

DeVilliers, Les (1995). *In Sight of Surrender: The U.S. Sanctions Campaign Against South Africa 1946–1993.* Westport, CT: Greenwood Press.

Diamond, Peter (1999, September). "What Stock Market Returns to Expect for the Future." Center for Retirement Research at Boston College Working Paper.

Dobris, J. (1986). "Arguments in Favour of Fiduciary Divestment of South African Securities." *Nebraska Law Review* 65: 209–23.

"Divestment Upheld" (1990). *Harvard Law Review* 103: 817–22.

Dowell, G., S. Hart, and B. Yeung (2000). "Do Corporate Global Environmental Standards Create or Destroy Market Value?" *Management Science* 46 (8): 1059–74.

*Economist* (2006). "Battling for Corporate America." March 11: 69–71.

—— (2007). "Activist Owners." June 2: 15.

Environmental Protection Agency (EPA) (2000). "Green Dividends: The Relationship between Firms' Environmental Performance and Financial Performance." EPA Study, Washington, DC.

Employee Benefit Research Institute (EBRI) (2007, June). "Recent Trends in Retirement Plan in the United States over the Past Quarter Century." Report. Washington, DC.

Fama, E. F. (1965). "The Behavior of Stock Market Prices." *Journal of Business* 38: 34–105.

*Financial Times* (2003a). May 15: 1.

—— (2003b). October 22.

Freshfields Bruckhaus Deringer (2005). "A Legal Framework for the Integration of Environmental, Social and Governance Issues into Institutional Investment." Report. UNEP Financial Initiative, New York.

Friedman, Milton (1970). "The Social Responsibility of Business Is to Increase Its Profits." *New York Times Magazine,* September 13. Available at http://www.colorado.edu/studentgroups/libertarians/issues/friedman-soc-resp-business.html. Accessed February 13, 2008.

Galbraith, John Kenneth (1969). *The New Industrial State.* Boston: Houghton Mifflin Company.

Gaskin, Russell (1998)." The Vigilante Investor, The Rise of Socially Responsible Investing as a Tool for Corporate Responsibility." *Development* 41: 81–85.

Ghilarducci, Teresa (1992). *Labor's Capital: The Economics and Politics of Private Pensions.* Cambridge, MA: MIT Press.

Global Reporting Initiative (GRI) (2006). Available at http://www.globalreporting.org/Home/. Accessed October 28, 2007.

Gluck, Kimberly, and Ying Becker (2005). "Can Environmental Factors Improve Stock Selection?" *Journal of Asset Management* 5 (4): 220–22.

Gompers, Paul, Joy L. Ishii, and Andrew Metrick (2003). "Corporate Governance and Equity Prices." *Quarterly Journal of Economics.* MIT Press, 118 (1): 107–55.

Gore, Al (2006). *An Inconvenient Truth.* New York: Rodale.

Graham, Benjamin, and David Dodd (2003). *Graham and Dodd's Security Analysis.* 6th ed. London: McGraw-Hill.

Grabher, G. (1993). *The Embedded Firm: On the Socio-economics of Industrial Networks.* London: Routledge.

Griffen, Jennifer J., and John Mahon (1997). "The Corporate Social Performance and Corporate Financial Performance Debate: Twenty-Five Years of Incomparable Research." *Business and Society* 36 (1): 5–31.

Guerard, John (1997). "Is There a Cost to Socially Responsible Investing?" *Journal of Investing* (Summer): 11–18.

Hansmann, Henry, and Reiner Kraakman (2002). "Toward a Single Model of Corporate Governance?" In *Corporate Governance Regimes: Convergence and Diversity,* ed. J. A. McCahery, P. Moerland, T. Raaijmakers, and L. Renneboog, 56–82. Oxford: Oxford University Press.

Harber, Wayne (2003). Private interview. London, October 7.

Harrigan, Sean (2003). Private interview. Sacramento, August 22.

Hawley, James P., and Andrew T. Williams (2000). *The Rise of Fiduciary Capitalism.* Philadelphia: University of Pennsylvania Press.

—— (2007). "Universal Owners: Challenges and Opportunities." *International Review of Corporate Governance* 15 (3): 415–20.

Hazlitt, William (1824). "On Corporate Bodies." *Table Talk.* 1952 ed. cited, London: Everyman Edition.

Herman, Edward S. (1981). *Corporate Control, Corporate Power.* Cambridge, UK: Cambridge University Press.

Hirschman, Albert O. (1970). *Exit, Voice, and Loyalty.* Cambridge, MA: Harvard University Press.

Hoffman, Andrew J. (1996). "A Strategic Response to Investor Activism." *Sloan Management Review* 37 (2) (Winter): 51–64.

Hurst, James W. (1970). *The Legitimacy of the Business Corporation in the Law of the United States, 1780–1970.* Charlottesville: University of Virginia Press.

ISS (2007). Institutional Shareholder Services. Available at http://www.issproxy.com/knowledge/environmental_social_governance.html. Accessed June 15, 2007.

Jarrell, Greg, K. Lehn, and W. Marr (1985). "Institutional Ownership, Tender Offers, and Long-Term Investments." Office of the Chief Economist, Securities and Exchange Commission, New York.

Jensen, Michael, and W. Meckling (1976). "Theory of the Firm: Managerial Behavior, Agency Costs, and Ownership Structure." *Journal of Financial Economics* 3 (4): 305–60.

Junkin, Andrew, and Thomas Toth (2006, July). "The CalPERS Effect on Targeted Company Share Prices." Wilshire and Associates Report, Santa Monica.

Kiernan, Matthew, and Jonathan Levinson (1998). "Environment Drives Financial Performance: The Jury Is In." *Environmental Quality Management* 7: 1–7.

Kinder, Peter (2004, June). "Pension Funds and the Companies They Own: New fiduciary duties in a changing social environment." Paper presented at a conference Socially Responsible Investing and Pension Funds Conference, American Enterprise Institute, Washington, DC.

La Porta, R., F. Lopez-De-Silanes, and A. Shleifer (1999). "Corporate Ownership around the World." *Journal of Finance* 54 (2): 471–517.

La Porta, R., F. Lopez-De-Silanes, A. Shleifer, and R. W. Vishny (1997). "Legal Determinants of External Finance." *Journal of Finance* 42 (3): 1131–50.

—— (1998). "Law and Finance." *Journal of Political Economy* 106 (6): 1113–55.

Lydenberg, Steven D. (2007). "Universal Investors and Socially Responsible Investors: A Tale of Two Emerging Affinities." *International Review of Corporate Governance* 15 (3): 467–77.

Majunder, S. (1994). The Long Term Orientation of Institutional Investors. University of Texas Working Paper, Austin.

Mansley, Mark, and Andrew Dlugolecki (2001). "Climate Change—A Risk Management Challenge for Institutional Investors." Universities Superannuation Scheme, London.

Margolis, Joshua, and James Walsh (2001). "Misery Loves Companies: Whither Social Initiatives by Business." Aspen Institute Working Paper.

Marsh, P. (1990). "Short-Termism on Trial." Institutional Fund Managers Association, London.

Maug, E. (1999). "How Effective Is Proxy Voting? Information Aggregation and Conflict Resolution in Corporate Voting Contests." Fuqua Business School Working Paper, Duke University, Durham, NC.

Mathieu, E. (2000). "Response of UK Pension Funds to the SRI Disclosure Regulation." Report. UK Social Investment Forum, London.

McConnell, J., and C. Muscarella (1985). "Corporate Capital Expenditure Decisions and the Market Value of the Firm." *Journal of Financial Economics* 14 (3): 399–422.

McKinsey (2002). "Global Investor Opinion Survey." Available at http://www.mckinsey.com. Accessed February 15, 2008.

*Memphis Business Journal* (2000). January 14.

Monks, Robert A. G. (1994). "Sears Case Study." Available at http://www.lens-library.com/info/sstan.html. Accessed February 15, 2008.

—— (1995, May). "Corporate Governance and Pension Plans: Positioning for the Year 2000." Paper presented at the Wharton Impact Conference, Wharton School, University of Pennsylvania.

—— (2001). *The New Global Investors*. Oxford, UK: Capstone.

Moon, P. (2003). Private Interview. London, July 4.

Nesbitt, S. L. (1994). "Long-Term Rewards from Shareholder Activism: A Study of the 'CalPERS Effect.'" *Journal of Applied Corporate Finance* 6 (Winter): 75–80.

—— (1995). The "CalPERS Effect": A Corporate Governance Update, July 19.

O'Barr, William M., and John M. Conley (1992). *Fortune and Folly, the Wealth and Power of Institutional Investing*. Homewood, IL: Business One Irwin.

Organization for Economic Cooperation and Development (OECD) (2004). "Principles of Corporate Governance." OECD Report. Available at http://www.oecd.org/document/22/0,2340,en_2649_201185_31558102_1_1_1_1,00.html.

Parkinson, John (1993). *Corporate Power and Responsibility*. Oxford: Clarendon Press.

Pava, Moses L., and Joshua Krausz (1995). *The Association Between Corporate Social Responsibility and Financial Performance: The Paradox of Social Cost*. Westport, CT: Quorum Books.

Pensions and Investments (2002). Databook, Crain Publishing. Chicago, December 31.

—— (2003). Databook, Crain Publishing. Chicago, December 31.

—— (2006). Databook, Crain Publishing. Chicago, December 25.

—— (2007). P&I 1,000: The Largest Retirement Plans, Crain Publishing. Chicago, January 22.

Porter, Michael (1995). "Green and Competitive—Ending the Stalemate." *Harvard Business Review* 73 (5): 120–34.

PricewaterhouseCoopers (2001). "The Opacity Index." Available at http://www.countryrisk.com/guide/archives/000088.html. Accessed February 17, 2008.

Reich, Robert (1998). "The New Meaning of Corporate Social Responsibility." *California Management Review* 40 (2): 8–17.

Reynolds, Thomas H., and Arturo A. Flores (1993). *Foreign Law: Current Sources of Codes and Legislation in Jurisdictions of the World*. Littleton, CO: F. B. Rothman.

Roe, Mark (1994). *Strong Managers, Weak Owners: The Political Roots of American Corporate Finance*. Princeton: Princeton University Press.

—— (2000). "Political Preconditions to Separating Ownership for Corporate Control." *Stanford Law Review* 53 (3): 539–606.

—— (2001). "Comparative Corporate Governance." In *Palgrave Dictionary of Law and Economics*. New York: Palgrave.

Romano, Roberta (2001). "Less Is More: Making Institutional Investor Activism a Valuable Mechanism of Corporate Governance." *Yale Journal on Regulation* 18 (2): 174–252.

Rondinelli, Dennis, and Gyula Vastag (1996). "International Environmental Standards and Corporate Policies." *California Management Review* 39(1): 106–22.

Shiller, Robert J. (2000). *Irrational Exuberance.* Princeton: Princeton University Press.

—— (2002). "Bubbles, Human Judgement and Expert Opinion." *Financial Analysts Journal* 58 (3): 18–27.

Shleifer, A. (1985). "A Theory of Yardstick Competition." *Rand Journal of Economics* 16 (3): 319–27.

Shleifer, A., and R. W. Vishny (1988). "Value Maximization and the Acquisition Process." *Journal of Economic Perspectives* 2 (1): 7–20.

—— (1997). "A Survey of Corporate Governance." *Journal of Finance* 52 (2): 737–83.

Simon, John G., Charles W. Powers, and Jon P. Gunnemann (1972). *The Ethical Investor: Universities and Corporate Responsibility.* New Haven, CT: Yale University Press.

Smith, Adam (1776). *The Wealth of Nations.* London: Everyman Edition.

Smith, M. P. (1996). "Shareholder Activism by Institutional Investors: Evidence from CalPERS." *Journal of Finance* 51 (1): 227–52.

Smith, N. Craig (1990). *Morality and the Market.* London: Routledge.

—— (2003). "Corporate Social Responsibility: Whether or How?" *California Management Review* 45 (4): 52–76.

Social Investment Forum (2006). "Ten Year Trends in Social Investing." 2005 Report on Socially Responsible Investing Trends in the United States. Washington, DC. Available at http://www.socialinvest.org/resources/pubs/. Accessed February 17, 2008.

—— (2007). The Social Investment Forum's 2006–2007 Annual Report. Available at http://www.socialinvest.org/resources/sriguide. Accessed February 17, 2008.

Stiglitz, Joseph E. (2002). *Globalization and Its Discontents.* New York: Norton.

Sudan Divestment Task Force (2007). "Interactive State Divestment Map." Available at http://www.sudandivestment.org/home.asp. Accessed July 5, 2007.

Tagliabue, J. (2000). "The French Are Resisting American Funds and Investors." *New York Times,* January 9.

Thamotheram, R. (2003). Private Interview. London, March 3.

Thamotheram, R., and Wildsmith, H. (2007). "Increasing Long Term Market Returns." *International Review of Corporate Governance* 15 (3): 438–54.

United Nations Environmental Program (UNEP) (2001). "Buried Treasure: Uncovering the Business Case for Corporate Sustainability." London.

—— (2002a). "Trust Us: The Global Reporters 2002 Survey of Corporate Sustainability Reporting." London, Sustainability. Available at http://www.sustainability.com/insight/article.asp?id=131. Accessed February 17, 2008.

—— (2002b, August). "Johannesburg World Summit on Sustainability." UNEP Report.

—— (2007). "UN Principles for Responsible Investing." Available at http://www.unpri.org.

United Kingdom, Parliament (1999). "The Occupational Pension Schemes (Investment, and Assignment, Forfeiture, Bankruptcy etc.)." Amendment 1999, statute no. 1849.

U.S. PBGC (2007). Pension Benefit Guaranty Corporation, "Pension Insurance Data Book 2006," Available at http://www.pbgc.gov/docs/2006databook.

U.S. Senate (2002, July). "The Role of the Board of Directors in Enron's Collapse." Report of the Permanent Subcommittee on Investigation of the Committee of Governmental Affairs, United States Senate no. 107–70), 54.

University Superannuation Scheme (2003). "Managing Pension Fund Assets as if the Long Term Really Did Matter." Competition Entries. Available at http://www.usshq.co.uk/special_interest_groups_index.php?name=SPECIAL_INTEREST_GROUPS_COMPETITION. Accessed February 17, 2008.

White, Ted (2003). Private Interview. Sacramento, January 15.

Williamson, Oliver E. (1985). *The Economic Institutions of Capitalism.* New York: Free Press.

World Bank (2003). *World Development Report 2003: Sustainable Development in a Dynamic World: Transforming Institutions, Growth, and Quality of Life,* Oxford: Oxford University Press.

# Index

# About the Author

## Tessa Hebb

Tessa Hebb is the Director of the Carleton Centre for Community Innovation, Carleton University, Canada. Her research focuses on the financial and extra-financial impact of pension fund investment. In 2008 she was awarded a multi-year research grant by the Social Sciences and Humanities Research Council, Government of Canada to further her work on responsible investing and corporate engagement. The Carleton Centre for Community Innovation is a leading knowledge producer on social finance tools and instruments.

Tessa Hebb is also a senior research associate at the Labor and Worklife Program, Harvard Law School and the Oxford University Centre for the Environment. She is researching the role of U.S. public sector pension funds and urban revitalization as lead investigator on a multi-year Rockefeller and Ford Foundation grant.

Her dissertation examined the impact of pension fund corporate engagement on the corporate governance, social and environmental standards of firm behavior. She was a Clarendon Scholar at Oxford University and was awarded the prestigious William E. Taylor Fellowship (2003) from the Social Sciences and Humanities Research Council of Canada. Tessa Hebb is also a recipient of the York University Schulich School of Business National Research in Financial Services and Public Policy Scholarship, Canada.

Tessa Hebb has published many articles on pension fund investing policies and is the co-editor of the volume *Working Capital the Power of Labor's Pensions* published by Cornell University Press (2001).